PRAISE FOR PREVIOUS EDITIONS

" . . . an asset to any wilderness traveler. Even if you've never used a compass or a GPS receiver before, you'll have a good understanding of the process after reading this book."
—Will Gadd, champion ice climber and author of *Ice & Mixed Climbing: Modern Technique*

"An ideal book for those who aspire to travel with precision in the backcountry."
—*Lewiston Morning Tribune*

"An informative book on how to walk in the woods."
—*Reel News*

"If you're planning a wilderness excursion, swallow your pride and pick up *Wilderness Navigation.*"
—*Pittsburgh Tribune-Review*

"Required reading for anyone who spends time in the outdoors with a map and compass."
—*St. Paul Pioneer Press*

". . . essentials for using a map and a compass as well as easy and practical techniques for using global positioning devices."
—*The News-Herald* (Willoughby, Ohio)

" . . . a great resource."
—*The Post Register* (Idaho Falls)

"Easy-to-understand instruction on map-reading and compass use."
—*Outside Bozeman*

WILDERNESS Navigation

mountaineers outdoor basics

Finding Your Way Using Map, Compass, Altimeter & GPS

Third Edition

Bob Burns
Mike Burns

MOUNTAINEERS
BOOKS

To the memories of the teachers of navigation who have gone before us, including Clinton M. Kelley, Richard B. Kaylor, Erhard Wichert, and Scott Fischer. Without their knowledge and leadership, some of us would still be lost in the wilderness.

Mountaineers Books is the publishing division of The Mountaineers, an organization founded in 1906 and dedicated to the exploration, preservation, and enjoyment of outdoor and wilderness areas.

MOUNTAINEERS BOOKS   1001 SW Klickitat Way, Suite 201, Seattle, WA 98134
800.553.4453, www.mountaineersbooks.org

Copyright © 2015 by Bob Burns and Mike Burns
All rights reserved. No part of this book may be reproduced or utilized in any form, or by any electronic, mechanical, or other means, without the prior written permission of the publisher.

Printed in the United States of America
Distributed in the United Kingdom by Cordee, www.cordee.co.uk
First edition, 1999. Second edition, 2004. Third edition: first printing 2015, seventh printing 2021

Copyeditor: Jane Crosen
Design: Mountaineers Books
Layout: Jen Grable
Illustrations: Jennifer Shontz, www.redshoedesign.com.
Figures 1, 8, 9, 10, 20–22, 24, 25, 27, 29, 30, 32, and 41 were taken directly from or adapted with minor modifications from *Mountaineering: The Freedom of the Hills, 8th Edition*. Figures 16 and 18 were adapted from *Freedom* but with major modifications. Figure 51 was adapted from the ninth edition of *Freedom*.
All photos by the authors unless otherwise indicated.
Cover photograph: *Silva Explorer Pro compass and Green Trails Mount Olympus Climbing Map* (Photo by Bob Burns)

Library of Congress Cataloging-in-Publication Data
Burns, Bob, 1942–
    Wilderness navigation : finding your way using map, compass, altimeter & gps / Bob Burns and Mike Burns.—Third edition.
        pages cm.
    Includes bibliographical references and index.
    ISBN 978-1-59485-945-8 (pbk.)—ISBN 978-1-59485-946-5 (ebook)
    1. Orienteering—Equipment and supplies. 2. Navigation—Equipment and supplies. 3. Outdoor recreation—Equipment and supplies. I. Burns, Mike, 1970– II. Title.
    GV200.4.B87 2015
    796.58—dc23

                                    2014034380

ISBN (paperback): 978-1-59485-945-8
ISBN (ebook): 978-1-59485-946-5

Contents

Preface

The origins of this book are lost among the rough notes of The Mountaineers' first climbing course, held in 1934. They were eventually published in 1960 as *Mountaineering: The Freedom of the Hills,* a comprehensive mountain climbing book containing information on equipment, navigation, wilderness travel, and technical details of climbing on rock, snow, and glaciers. It has been revised eight times since its initial publication, and we have contributed to the last six revisions.

In addition to writing about navigation, we have hiked, scrambled, snowshoed, and climbed extensively, as well as taught navigation in courses sponsored by The Mountaineers and Green Trails Maps. In some of the nonclimbing classes, we have often been asked to recommend a book covering the material presented in our courses and lectures. However, the only book using the same methods and covering the same material as these courses was *Freedom.* Some skiers, snowshoers, and hikers balked at buying a large, expensive book filled with details of technical rock and ice climbing just to obtain information on navigation; it was out of this need that the idea for *Wilderness Navigation* emerged.

This book was originally envisioned as a concise book containing the same information covered in the navigation chapter of *Freedom.* However, much useful information had been excluded from *Freedom* in order to keep its size manageable. *Wilderness Navigation* was therefore expanded, with the addition of considerable technical information as well as material on wilderness routefinding. This book now provides more than twice as much material as the navigation chapter in *Freedom.*

The methods of using maps and compasses in this book have been taught for many years by The Mountaineers. When using the methods explained in this book, orienting the map is not necessary, nor is it necessary to add or subtract declination, nor to draw declination lines on your maps. Instead, we encourage the use of compasses with adjustable declination and explain how to make all compasses work like such compasses. This has proven to be an easy and dependable method of dealing with declination.

Since the publication of the second edition in 2004, we have received from readers a number of suggestions for improvement. We have incorporated many of these into this third edition, including an update to the descriptions of presently available maps, compasses, altimeters, and Global Positioning System (GPS) devices, as well as updated declination maps for the United States and the world. Since 2004 there have also been some important changes to the GPS, requiring updates to that chapter, including the interfacing of the GPS receiver with the home computer, as well as using the GPS function in smart phones. We have also added more information on navigational techniques, as well as websites and other sources containing useful navigational information.

Since the third edition was published in 2015, there have been changes in the natural magnetic world, as well as in navigational technology and the devices used for wilderness navigation. Major modifications in this latest printing include: significant changes to the topographical maps produced by the US Geological Survey, changes in magnetic declination indicated on maps of the US, changes to be consistent with the ninth edition of *Mountaineering: The Freedom of the Hills*, and the development of navigational products. We have also made numerous minor changes throughout in response to questions and suggestions from readers, to offer increased clarity and eliminate ambiguity. We hope that these updates will enhance the book's usefulness. We invite any reader with questions, comments, or suggestions for improvement to write or email Mountaineers Books.

Acknowledgments

We wish to express our appreciation to a number of individuals who have contributed to this book. We are grateful to our friend Ronald Gailis for his research into sources of information on geomagnetism and GPS, as well as his assistance and suggestions during the writing of this book. We also wish to thank John Bell for his significant contributions to the navigation chapter of the eighth and ninth editions of *Mountaineering: The Freedom of the Hills.*

We also thank the staff of Mountaineers Books, particularly Margaret Sullivan and Laura Shauger. Finally, a thank-you to Peter Hendrickson, former chairman of The Mountaineers' Navigation Committee, for his many helpful and constructive suggestions for improvement of this book, which is required reading for The Mountaineers' navigation course.

Introduction

Where am I? How far is it to my destination? Will I be able to find my way back? This book shows you how to use orientation and navigation to answer these most frequently asked questions in wilderness travel.

By the time you finish reading this guide, you will have a good handle on the tools of navigation and the proven techniques of top-notch navigators, who have acquired their skills through years of roaming—and being lost in—the wilderness. You will have the basic knowledge to head into the wilds, work out the way to your destination, and, most importantly, find your way home.

The tools and techniques are simple and straightforward—but exacting. Study them carefully to help make your wilderness adventures successful and to keep you safe and within the ranks of surviving navigators. Before you immerse yourself in this book, remember navigation is easy and fun. (So much fun, in fact, that some people engage in *orienteering,* in which participants compete using a map and compass to get to various destinations on structured courses.) First, a few definitions:

Orientation is the science of determining your exact position on Earth. People who spend a reasonable amount of time and effort usually gain these skills, even if they have little background or interest in math or science.

Navigation is the science of determining the location of your objective and keeping yourself pointed in the right direction from your starting point to this destination. Like orientation, navigation is a required skill for all wilderness travelers.

Routefinding is the art of selecting and following the best path appropriate for the abilities and equipment of the party. It takes a lot to be a good routefinder: an integrated sense of terrain, as well as a combination of good judgment, experience, acute awareness, and instinct. In addition to a solid foundation in the orientation and navigation skills described in the following chapters, wilderness routefinding also requires considerable time, practice, and experience.

The route through this book is divided into two parts. The first, consisting of chapters 1 through 5, contains basic information on maps, compasses, orientation, navigation, how to avoid getting lost, and what to do if you *do* get lost. These chapters contain the basic essentials of wilderness navigation for all wilderness travelers, including those who never intend to leave a well-maintained trail.

Chapters 6 through 10 provide more detailed information on wilderness navigation: the latitude/longitude and UTM coordinate systems; distance measurement and pace; the use of clinometers, altimeters, GPS receivers, and smartphones; and wilderness routefinding on trails, in the forest, desert, in alpine areas, and on snow and glaciers. We recommend a careful reading of these chapters for anyone who intends to leave the trail and venture cross-country in search of hidden fishing lakes, challenging mountain peaks, interesting cross-country ski routes, and other destinations beyond the well-maintained trail.

If you do not own a compass, we suggest that you read at least through chapter 2 before buying one.

We also highly recommend that you complete the practice problems in the appendix as you navigate through this book.

This book will *not* make you an expert in wilderness navigation; only practice and experience will do so. But it *can* give you a basic foundation in the skills necessary for safe and enjoyable wilderness travel.

A NOTE ABOUT SAFETY

Safety is an important concern in all outdoor activities. No book can alert you to every hazard or anticipate the limitations of every reader. The descriptions of techniques and procedures in this book are intended to provide general information. This is not a complete text on wilderness travel. Nothing substitutes for formal instruction, routine practice, and plenty of experience. When you follow any of the procedures described here, you assume responsibility for your own safety. Use this book as a general guide to further information. Under normal conditions, excursions into the backcountry require attention to traffic, road and trail conditions, weather, terrain, the capabilities of your party, and other factors. Keeping informed on current conditions and exercising common sense are the keys to a safe, enjoyable outing.

—*Mountaineers Books*

Map Basics

CHAPTER OBJECTIVES

- Learn basic map terminology.
- Understand how to read topographic maps, including declination, north–south reference lines, colors, contour lines, and slope direction.
- Discover the limitations of maps.
- Customize and prepare maps for wilderness trips.
- Find out where to get maps.

A map is a symbolic picture of a place. In convenient shorthand, it conveys a phenomenal amount of information in a form that is easy to understand and easy to carry. For water activities, navigational charts provide the same level of information as topographic maps do on land, but with particular attention to navigational hazards. No one should venture into the wilderness without a map or chart of the area, or without the skills required to interpret and thoroughly understand it.

You can find a lot of useful information on a map. For wilderness land travel, the most important items are topographic features, vegetation, and elevation information, which are discussed in this chapter. (See chapter 6 for more in-depth information, such as the use of the latitude/longitude and UTM coordinate systems, distance and slope measurement, and surveying information.) Note the publication date of the map and obtain the latest information, because roads, trails, and other features may have changed since the map was printed.

UNDERSTANDING MAP TYPES AND TERMS

It will be helpful to start this discussion of maps with a description of how cartographers divide up Earth. The distance around our planet is divided into 360 units called **degrees** (designated with a ° symbol). A measurement east or west is called **longitude**. Longitude is measured from 0° to 180°, both east and west, starting at the Greenwich meridian running through the Royal Observatory, Greenwich, near London, England. A measurement north or south is called **latitude**. Latitude is measured from 0° to 90°, north and south, from the equator. New York City, for example, is situated at about 74 degrees west longitude and 41 degrees north latitude (74° W and 41° N). Each degree is divided into 60 units called **minutes** (designated with a ' symbol), and each minute is further subdivided into 60 **seconds** (designated with a " symbol). On a map, a latitude of 46 degrees, 53 minutes, and 15 seconds north would be written like this: N46°53'15". Alternatively, this can be written as 46 degrees, 53.25 minutes, or 46.8875 degrees (more about this in chapter 6). The latter expression, referred to as degrees and decimal degrees, is most commonly used by search-and-rescue groups.

Another commonly used position reference system is the **Universal Transverse Mercator (UTM)** system, based on the metric system. This is often used with GPS receivers and is discussed in detail in chapter 6, along with more detail on using the latitude/longitude system with marine charts.

The **scale** of a map is a ratio between measurements on the map and measurements in the real world. A common way to state the scale is to compare a map measurement with a ground measurement (as in 1 inch equals 1 mile) or to give a specific mathematical ratio (as in the 1:24,000 scale most commonly used in the United States, where any one unit of measure on the map equals 24,000 units of the same measure on Earth). The scale is shown graphically, usually at the bottom of the map.

Several different types of maps are available:

Relief maps attempt to show terrain in three dimensions by using various shades of green, gray, and brown, terrain sketching, and raised surfaces. They help in visualizing the ups and downs of the landscape and have some value in trip planning. Relief maps are often displayed at visitors' centers in national parks and recreation areas.

Land management and recreation maps, published by the US Forest Service, the National Park Service, other government agencies, and timber companies, are frequently updated and thus are very useful for current details on roads, trails, ranger stations, and other works of the human hand. They usually show only the horizontal relationship of natural features, without the contour lines that indicate the shape of the land. These maps are often quite helpful for trip planning.

Sketch maps tend to be crudely drawn but often make up in specialized route detail what they lack in draftsmanship. Such drawings can be effective supplements to other map and guidebook information.

Guidebook maps vary greatly in quality. Some are merely sketches, while others are accurate modifications of topographic maps. They often contain useful details on roads, trails, and wilderness routes.

Topographic maps are the best of all for wilderness travelers. They depict topography, the shape of Earth's surface, by showing **contour lines** that represent constant elevations above and below sea level. These maps, essential to off-trail travel, are produced in many countries. They should be brought along on all wilderness excursions, along with any of the above-mentioned maps. Some are produced by government agencies, such as the US Geological Survey (USGS), whereas others are printed by private companies. Some private companies produce maps based on USGS maps and update them with recent trail and road details, sometimes combining sections of different USGS maps into one. One example of such a company is Green Trails, Inc., which makes maps for mountainous areas in the Pacific Northwest and a few other areas. These maps are often useful supplements to standard topographic maps and are particularly helpful for trail hiking.

As an example of topographic maps, we will look in detail at the USGS maps.

USGS TOPOGRAPHIC MAPS

One type of USGS map commonly used by wilderness travelers covers an area of 7.5 minutes (that is, $1/8$ degree) of latitude by 7.5 minutes of longitude. These maps are known as the **7.5-minute series**. An older type of USGS map covers an area of 15 minutes (that is, $1/4$ degree) of latitude by 15 minutes of longitude. These maps are part of what is called the **15-minute series**. Four 7.5-minute maps are needed to cover the same area as one 15-minute map.

The 7.5-minute map is the standard for the contiguous United States and Hawaii and is the most commonly used type for wilderness travelers in the United States outside of Alaska.

- The scale is 1:24,000, or roughly 2.5 inches to the mile, or 4 centimeters (cm) to the kilometer (km).
- Each map covers an area of approximately 6 by 9 miles (9 by 14 km), and the UTM squares are one kilometer (km) on a side.

The 15-minute map is the standard only for Alaska, due to its immense size.

- The scale is 1:63,360, or exactly 1 inch to 1 mile, or 1.6 cm to 1 km. The north–south extent of each Alaska map is 15 minutes, but the east–west extent is greater than 15 minutes, because the lines of longitude converge toward the North Pole.
- Each map covers an area of about 12 to 16 miles (19 by 26 km) east–west and 18 miles (28 km) north–south.

Descriptions of the latitude/longitude and UTM systems are given in chapter 6. What follows in this chapter is a description of basic topographic map features of most interest to wilderness travelers.

TIP: In Canada and most of the rest of the world where the metric system is used, the most commonly used comparable scale is 1:50,000. Scales of 1:25,000 and others are occasionally used as well.

TOPOGRAPHIC MAP FEATURES

Each USGS map is referred to as a quadrangle (or quad) and covers an area bounded on the north and south by latitude lines that differ by an amount equal to the map series (7.5 minutes or 15 minutes) and on the east and west by longitude lines that differ by the same amount, except for Alaska.

The USGS currently provides two types of topographic maps for the United States: historical maps (last updated prior to 2010) and the new US Topo series. Though some historical maps are not fully updated with regard to roads, logging activity, and structures, they are nevertheless useful for topography, trails, and other features of interest to the wilderness traveler. They are sold at roughly half the cost of the US Topo maps. The US Topo maps are more up to date for depicting most human-caused features, but many do not yet show all trails, nor the elevations of mountain summits. Trails are being added to these maps as time allows, and so it may be years before all trails are shown on them. To read a topographic map, you'll need to know key map features such as colors, contour lines, and reference lines.

Colors

Colors on a USGS topographic map have specific meanings:

Red: Major roads and survey information.

Blue: Rivers, lakes, springs, waterfalls, marshes, glaciers, and permanent snowfields.

Black or gray: Minor roads, trails, railroads, buildings, benchmarks, UTM coordinates, and other human-related features.

Green: Solid green indicates a forest. A lack of green does not mean that an area is devoid of vegetation but simply that any growth is too small or scattered to show on the map. Contour lines and elevations of index contours are in brown.

White with blue contour lines (on historical USGS maps): A glacier or permanent snowfield. The contour lines are in solid blue, with their edges indicated by dashed blue lines. Elevations are shown in blue. **Rope up for all glacier travel!**

White with blue speckles (US Topo maps): Glaciers and permanent snowfields. Elevations and contour lines are shown in brown.

White with brown contour lines: Any area without substantial forest, such as a high alpine area, a clear-cut, a rockslide, an avalanche gully, or a meadow. Study the map for other clues.

Purple: Partial revision of an existing map.

Be sure to be aware of the temporal nature of these map features, since logging, glacial expansion or recession, and other changes might have occurred since the map was last updated.

Contour Lines

The heart of a topographic map is its overlay of **contour lines**, each line indicating a constant elevation as it follows the shape of the landscape. A map's *contour interval* is the difference in elevation between two adjacent contour lines. The contour interval is clearly printed at the bottom of the map. Every fifth contour line, called an *index contour*, is printed darker than the other lines and is labeled with the elevation.

One of the most important bits of information a topographic map reveals is whether you will be traveling uphill or downhill. If the route crosses lines of increasingly higher elevation, you will be going uphill. If it crosses lines of decreasing elevation, the route is downhill. Flat or

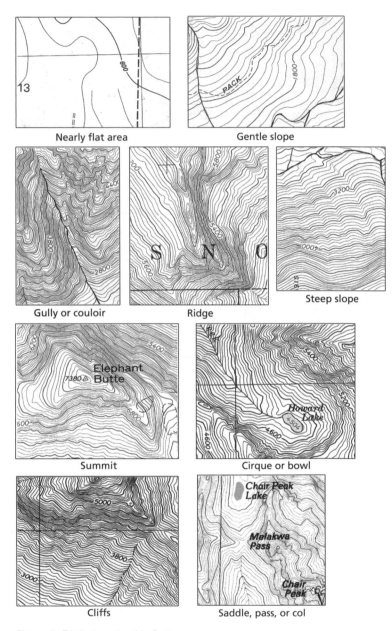

Figure 1. Basic topographic features

sidehill travel is indicated by a route that crosses no lines, remaining within a single contour interval.

Topographic maps also show cliffs, passes, summits, and other features (figure 1). Main features depicted by contour lines include the following:

Flat areas: No contour lines at all.

Gentle slopes: Widely spaced contour lines.

Steep slopes: Closely spaced contour lines.

Cliffs: Contour lines extremely close together or even touching.

Valleys, ravines, gullies, and couloirs: Contour lines in a pattern of Us for gentle, rounded valleys or gullies; Vs for sharp valleys and gullies. The Us and Vs point uphill, in the direction of higher elevation.

Ridges or spurs: Contour lines in a pattern of Us for gentle, rounded ridges; Vs for sharp ridges. The Us and Vs point downhill, in the direction of lower elevation.

Peaks or summits: A concentric pattern of contour lines, with the summit being the innermost and highest ring. Peaks are also often indicated by Xs, elevations, benchmarks (BMs), or triangle symbols.

Cirques or bowls: Patterns of contour lines forming at least a semicircle, rising from a low spot in the center to form a natural amphitheater at the head of a valley.

Saddles, passes, or cols: An hourglass shape (with higher contour lines on two sides), indicating a low point on a ridge.

> **TIP:** As you travel in the wilderness, frequently observe the terrain and associate its appearance with its depiction on the map. Note all the topographic features—such as ridges, gullies, streams, and summits—as you pass them. This helps you to maintain a close estimate of exactly where you are and helps you become an expert map reader.

You will get better and better at interpreting contour lines by comparing actual terrain with its representation on a map. The goal is to be able to glance at a topographic map and have a sharp mental image of just what the place will look like. There is no substitute for experience, so be sure to pay close attention to the appearance of various topographic features you see in the wilderness, and note their depiction on the topo map. Before you venture into the wilderness, we suggest that you carefully study figures 2 through 5 to gain an appreciation of how various features shown in photographs appear on topo maps.

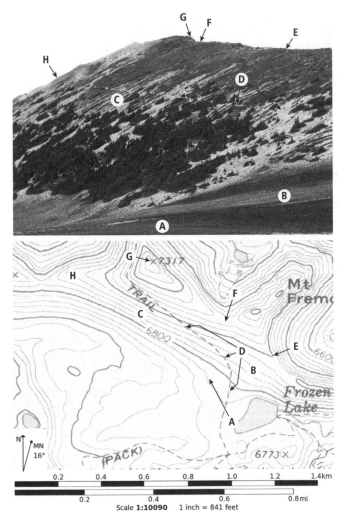

Figure 2. Photograph of a mountainous area and its depiction on a topographic map

A. Photo taken from here, in direction shown
B. Gentle slope
C. Moderate slope
D. Trail along hillside
E. Ridge crest
F. Saddle along ridge crest
G. Minor summit on ridge
H. Skyline ridge

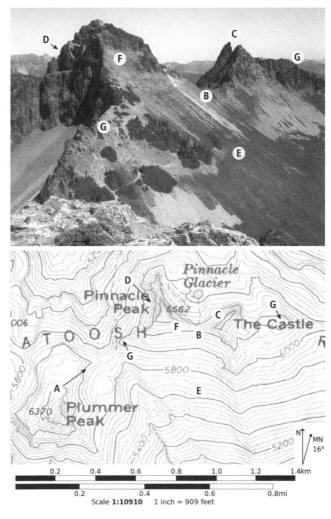

Figure 3. Photograph of mountain peaks and their depiction on a corresponding topographic map

A. Photograph taken from this location (in direction shown)
B. Saddle or col
C. Twin summits
D. Cliff
E. Moderate slope
F. Steep slope
G. Ridges

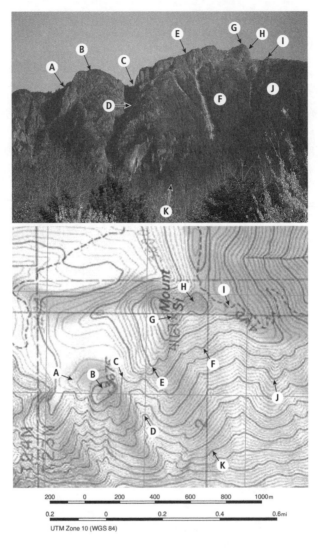

Figure 4. Photograph of a mountainous area and its depiction on a topographic map, illustrating various topographical features

A. Ridge crest
B. Secondary summit
C. Saddle (pass)
D. Major gully descending from saddle
E. Ridge crest

F. Broad ridge
G. Primary summit
H. Very steep slope
I. Nearly level area
J. Broad forested ridge
K. Direction of photograph

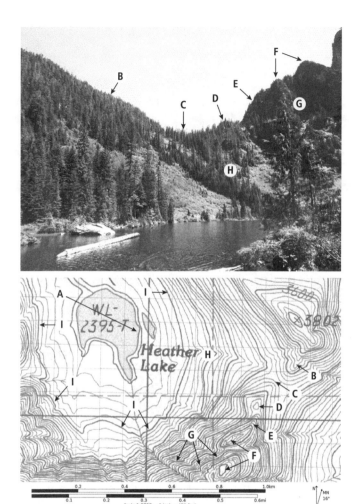

Figure 5. Photograph of a mountain cirque and its depiction on a topographic map

A. *Photograph taken from here (in direction shown)*

B. *Moderately steep (30°) ridge*

C. *Low point on ridge (saddle); note hourglass-shaped pattern of contour lines on topo map.*

D. *Small forested knoll*

E. *Steep (60°) ridge*

F. *Pinnacles*

G. *Very steep cliffs below pinnacles*

H. *Broad gully between saddle and lake*

I. *Note contour line nearly encircling lake; classic characteristics of a cirque (not shown in photo).*

REMEMBERING HOW TO IDENTIFY RIDGES AND GULLIES ON MAPS

If you ever forget whether upward-pointing or downward-pointing contour lines indicate ridges or gullies, just remember that **streams usually flow down gullies**, and not on ridges. So if you have a map of a hilly or mountainous area, find a thin blue line indicating a stream, and examine the contour lines around it. The upward-pointing contour lines will remind you that they indicate a gully.

Declination Information

The margins of USGS maps contain important information, such as the date of publication and revision, contour intervals, map scales, and the area's **magnetic declination** at the time the map was last updated, which is the difference between true north and magnetic north. Declination is extremely important and will be discussed in more detail in chapter 2. Depending on when the map was printed, declination is labeled differently.

- USGS historical topo maps printed in 1988 or later (see figure 6A) have a statement such as "1990 Magnetic North Declination 20° EAST."
- USGS historical maps printed before 1988 and the newer US Topo maps usually have a declination diagram printed at the bottom of the map (see figure 6B). The star indicates true north and the "MN" indicates magnetic north. The angle difference between these two is the magnetic declination for that area at the time the map was last updated.

North–South Reference Lines

Lines running north–south on the map are very important for using the map and compass together, as will be explained in chapter 2. Some maps have a grid of **UTM (Universal Transverse Mercator) lines** printed on the map, and these can be used as north–south reference lines. North is usually at the top of the map, unless otherwise indicated.

Maps printed in 1988 or later usually have a grid of black lines representing the 1000-meter intervals of the UTM grid (see figure 6A). This grid is usually slightly offset from true north, because the map

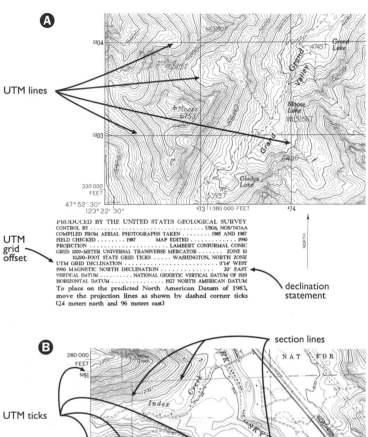

A

UTM lines

UTM grid offset

PRODUCED BY THE UNITED STATES GEOLOGICAL SURVEY
CONTROL BY . . . . USGS, NOS/NOAA
COMPILED FROM AERIAL PHOTOGRAPHS TAKEN . . . . 1985 AND 1987
FIELD CHECKED 1987   MAP EDITED 1990
PROJECTION . . . . LAMBERT CONFORMAL CONIC
GRID: 1000-METER UNIVERSAL TRANSVERSE MERCATOR . . . . ZONE 10
      10,000-FOOT STATE GRID TICKS . . . . . WASHINGTON, NORTH ZONE
UTM GRID DECLINATION . . . . 0°14' WEST
1990 MAGNETIC NORTH DECLINATION . . . . 20° EAST
VERTICAL DATUM . . . . NATIONAL GEODETIC VERTICAL DATUM OF 1929
HORIZONTAL DATUM . . . . 1927 NORTH AMERICAN DATUM
To place on the predicted North American Datum of 1983,
move the projection lines as shown by dashed corner ticks
(24 meters north and 96 meters east)

declination statement

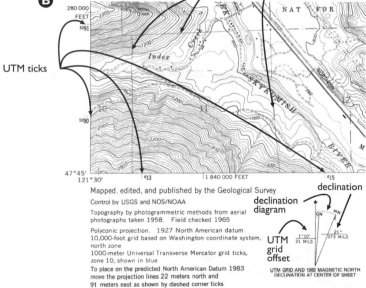

B

section lines

UTM ticks

Mapped, edited, and published by the Geological Survey
Control by USGS and NOS/NOAA
Topography by photogrammetric methods from aerial
photographs taken 1958. Field checked 1965
Polyconic projection. 1927 North American datum
10,000-foot grid based on Washington coordinate system,
north zone
1000-meter Universal Transverse Mercator grid ticks,
zone 10, shown in blue
To place on the predicted North American Datum 1983
move the projection lines 22 meters north and
91 meters east as shown by dashed corner ticks

declination diagram

declination

UTM grid offset

UTM GRID AND 1982 MAGNETIC NORTH
DECLINATION AT CENTER OF SHEET

*Figure 6. Lower left corner of USGS topographic maps: A. newer than 1988,
B. older than 1988*

is representing our spherical planet on a flat surface, and therefore is introducing a slight error. The amount of this offset is given in the lower left corner of the map such as "UTM GRID DECLINATION 0°14' WEST." The UTM grid is very helpful when using a GPS receiver (see chapter 9). These lines may also be used as a north–south reference (see chapter 2), but only if the offset of the grid is less than 1°. If the offset of the UTM grid is more than 1°, then you should use surveyors' section lines (usually printed in red). If the map has no section lines, if the section lines do not truly run north–south, or if the UTM grid lines are too faint (as on US Topo maps), you can **draw in your own north–south lines**.

Place one long edge of a long straightedge (such as a meter stick or a yardstick) along the left margin of the map and draw a line along the other side of the straightedge. Then move it over to the line you just drew and draw another line, and repeat.

This way, you will have a set of north–south lines that are truly north–south. This will help you achieve accuracy in measuring and plotting bearings on the map using your compass (see chapter 2).

On maps printed prior to 1988, UTM lines are usually not shown. However, there are faint (usually blue) **UTM "tick" marks** along the edges of such maps showing the locations of the 1000-meter lines (see figure 6B). The declination diagrams for these maps usually have a line to GN, meaning *grid north*. This is the offset of the UTM grid from true north. If this offset is less than 1°, then you can connect these tick marks on your table at home using a straightedge to place a UTM grid on the map, as explained above. You can then use these as north–south reference lines. However, if the amount of difference between true north and grid north is greater than 1°, then you should draw in your own north–south lines parallel with the edges of the map, as described above.

Direction of the Slope

Traveling along a contour line means traveling on a roughly level route with no slope. Conversely, traveling in the direction perpendicular (at a right angle) to a contour line means traveling directly uphill or downhill, sometimes called the *fall line.* Knowing this can be a valuable clue as to your position. You can easily find this direction on the map or in the field for any point on sloping terrain. This fact can be very useful in orientation, and we will refer to it in several places in this book. For example, in figure 7, point G has a slope that falls off to the southwest. Point H, on the other hand, has a slope falling off roughly to the east.

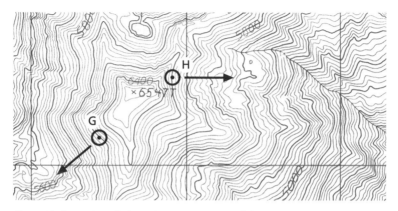

Figure 7. Examples of observing the direction of the slope on a map

We will be able to express this direction more precisely after we explain how to measure and plot bearings using the compass in chapter 2.

Using the direction of the slope cannot prove that you are at any particular place, but it can disprove it, and this can sometimes be a big help in trying to figure out where you are.

In figure 7, for example, suppose you have climbed Peak 6547 and have descended a few hundred feet. You wish to find out where you are, and you guess that you are at point G. That means that the slope should be falling off to the southwest. However, when standing on the slope and facing downhill, you see the midday sun on your right, so you know that you are facing roughly east. This proves that you cannot be at point G. You could very possibly be at point H, since at this point the slope falls off to the east. But there are other places where the slope falls off to the east, so you cannot prove that you are at point H.

KNOWING THE LIMITATIONS OF MAPS

Keep a couple of cautionary thoughts in mind as you study a topographic map. **The map will not show all the terrain features** that you actually see on your trip, because there is a limit to what mapmakers can cram onto the map without reducing it to an unreadable clutter. If a feature is not at least as high as the contour interval, it may not be shown, so a 30-foot cliff may come as a surprise when you are navigating with a map that has a 40-foot contour interval.

Check the date of the map, because topographic maps may not be revised very often, and information on forests and on roads and other works of the human hand or natural disaster (such as the eruption of a volcano) could be out of date. A forest may have been logged, a glacier may have advanced or receded, or a road may have been extended or closed since the last update. Although topographic maps are essential to wilderness travel, you often need to supplement them with information from visitors to the area, guidebooks, websites, and other maps.

> **TIP:** When you learn of changes (such as road or trail closures), you should note them on your map in pencil, along with the date.

CUSTOMIZING AND MODIFYING MAPS

Sometimes a trip runs through portions of two or more maps. Adjoining maps can be folded at the edges and brought together, or you can create your own customized map by cutting out the nonpertinent areas and splicing the rest together with tape. Maps can also be created by using a computer and readily available map software. When customizing maps, be sure to **include plenty of territory** so that you will have a good overview of the entire trip, including the surrounding area (which might be needed for orientation; see chapter 3).

Black-and-white photocopies are good for marking the route, but since they do not show colors, they should be used only as supplements to the real thing. If a durable, high-quality reproduction is needed, then a color photocopy onto waterproof paper with waterproof ink may be the best approach. Some outdoor recreation stores have the capability to produce computer-generated maps covering whatever area you want by combining various sections of USGS quadrangles. Though these customized maps are slightly more expensive than the standard USGS quadrangles, you may appreciate their convenience.

If you choose to cut off the white borders of your topo map to save weight and bulk, be sure to **retain all of the important information** at the bottom of the map, including the scale, contour interval, declination, datum, and UTM zone, even if such information may not seem important to you at the time. If you ever decide to use a GPS receiver, you may later regret having cut off and discarded this essential information.

CARRYING MAPS ON A WILDERNESS TRIP

One of the most important aspects of carrying a map is to do so in such a way that you can get to it at any time. We suggest that you carry it in your pocket.

TIP: Cargo pants or shorts with big pockets are excellent for carrying maps, compasses, and other objects that you want to access quickly and conveniently. It is a lot easier to make critical frequent observations if you can quickly get to your map at any time.

Map Folding

One good way to carry a map is to fold it to show the area where you will be traveling, and then enclose it in a clear plastic map case or a plastic ziplock bag. This way, it will be protected from the elements, always visible, easy to remove, and compact.

It is best to fold your map so that your entire route for a given leg of the trip will always be **visible without unfolding the map**, if possible. The folded map should also be slightly less than the size of a large cargo shorts or pants pocket (approximately 5 by 5 inches or 13 cm by 13 cm). With the finished dimension in mind, fold your map so that your starting point is on one edge of the folded map, and fold up the remaining part of the map so that as much of the route as possible is visible. At the main fold your route can continue to the other side of the map. It will then be very easy for you to flip your map over to the other side as your day progresses without the need to refold it.

TIP: Try to keep folds away from key route junctions or other important areas of interest, since folds tend to degrade with time and wear, particularly if the map gets wet.

Another way to keep your map accessible throughout your trip is to fold it to approximately the inner dimensions of your camera case, and carry it inside the case, held on the hip belt of your pack. Then you can easily check your location on your map or take an impromptu photo.

We recommend against laminating maps for your wilderness adventure, since doing so makes it difficult to fold or write on the map.

FINDING AND BUYING MAPS

Many outdoor recreation stores sell topographic maps, and some bookstores and nautical supply stores stock them as well. You can often find such stores by doing an internet search for "topographic maps for [your area or state]."

You can **order topographic maps** directly from the USGS by going to www.store.usgs.gov. If you do not know the name of the map for the area you need, you can view a **map locator** screen to find all the USGS maps available for the desired area. Select the map you want, and then **view, download, print, or purchase** many topographic maps from the USGS website. If you download topo maps, then you can print them out on your own printer, or you can bring a saved digital copy to a local print shop to get a larger hard copy of the map.

To obtain **topographic maps for Canada**, search online for "Map Distribution Centres" and other stores. Several examples are www .canmaps.com/topographic and www.mytopo.com.

Other internet map sources include www.caltopo.com (for topo maps of the entire United States, not just California), www.mytopo. com, and other websites found with an internet search. Keep in mind that your software-generated map will only be as good as allowed by your printer. We highly recommend getting a color printer if you choose to do this, since color is such an important part of any topo-graphic map. Furthermore, printing your own USGS map requires nine sheets of 8.5-by-11-inch paper to cover the same area as one 7.5-min-ute quadrangle map at the same scale. We recommend purchasing the USGS paper copy directly from the USGS, to get the highest-quality map with colorfast ink that will not run when wet. You can also check with any local outdoor clubs in your geographic area (e.g., The Moun-taineers, The Mazamas, The Sierra Club, the Colorado Mountain Club, and other organizations) to get recommendations for local map sources.

It is possible to purchase waterproof paper on which to print maps, but the inks used in many consumer-level printers are not waterproof, and the colors may run if such maps get wet. If you print your own maps, take extra care to keep them dry.

DIGITAL MAPS

You can download maps from the USGS and other sources and view them on your desktop, tablet, laptop, or smartphone. You can also use smartphone apps such as Gaia, Backcountry Navigator, and others. If you rely on an app for map data, you must also carry a backup paper map of the area so that you are never solely relying on an electronic device dependent on battery power.

CHAPTER SUMMARY

With the exception of your brain, a map is your most important naviga-tional tool. No one should venture into the wilderness without one, nor without the ability to interpret it. You should also have ready access to it, and should consult it frequently during your wilderness adventure. Note that the subtitle of this book is "Finding Your Way Using Map, Compass, Altimeter & GPS." The order of these words was chosen carefully to list these four items in order from highest to lowest priority: first, a map, then a compass, and so on.

SKILLS CHECK

- What do the terms *latitude, longitude,* and *degrees* mean?
- Where can you find declination information on a map?
- List three ways to find true north on a USGS map.
- What do a map's contour lines and colors show?
- Name two limitations of topographic maps.

PRACTICE PROBLEMS *See the appendix for problem instructions.*

- Problems 4 and 12 involve identifying elevations on a map.
- Problems 1, 9, and 22 involve identifying topographic features on a map.
- Problems 7 and 15 involve finding direction of a slope on a map.

Compass Basics

CHAPTER OBJECTIVES

- Learn the types of baseplate compasses.
- Cope with magnetic declination.
- Master the four basic steps of using a compass:
    1. Taking (measuring) bearings in the field
    2. Following bearings in the field
    3. Measuring (taking) bearings from a map
    4. Plotting (following) bearings on a map
- Cope with the pitfalls of using a compass.
- Practice using a compass.

This chapter lays the foundation for using the compass, and for using the map and compass together. Though these principles are easy to learn and apply, they are nevertheless crucial to successful operation of the compass, so we urge you to study them carefully. If you learn these well, you will become proficient in using the map and compass in the wilderness.

The compass is a very simple device that can do a wondrous thing: It can reveal at any time and any place exactly what direction it is pointing. On a simple wilderness trek in good weather, the compass may never leave your pack or pocket. But as the route becomes more complex or as the weather worsens, or if you are merely curious about identifying various features in your surroundings, it comes into its own as a critical tool of wilderness travel.

A **compass** is nothing more than a magnetized needle that responds to Earth's magnetic field. Compass makers have added a few things to this basic unit to make it easier to use. But stripped to the core, there is just that needle, aligned with Earth's magnetism, and from that known reference line we can determine any other direction.

TYPES OF BASEPLATE COMPASSES

The basic features (see figure 8A) of a **baseplate compass** to be used for wilderness travel include:

- A freely rotating magnetic needle—one end is a different color (usually red) from the other so you can tell which end points to north.
- A circular, rotating housing, capsule, or *bezel*, for the needle—filled with a fluid that dampens (reduces) the vibrations of the needle, making readings more accurate.
- A dial around the circumference of the housing—graduated clockwise in 1- or 2-degree increments, from 0° to 360°.
- An orienting arrow within the capsule, to align with the needle.
- A set of parallel meridian lines—located below the needle, which rotate with the bezel, separate from the baseplate.
- An index line—used to set and read bearings.
- A transparent, rectangular baseplate for the entire unit—including a direction-of-travel line (sometimes with an arrow at one end) to point toward your objective. The longer the baseplate, the more accurate your readings will be.

Optional features (see figure 8B) available on some compasses include:

- An adjustable declination arrow—an easy, dependable way to correct for magnetic declination; well worth the added cost.
- A sighting mirror—another way to improve accuracy.
- A ruler or rulers—calibrated in inches and/or millimeters, and/ or with latitude and longitude or UTM lines; used to measure short distances or to locate your position on a map.
- A clinometer—used to measure the angle of a slope in the field.
- A magnifying glass bubble—used to help read closely spaced contour lines and other details on maps.
- Roamer (sometimes spelled romer) scales to enable you to identify your position more precisely on topo maps with UTM

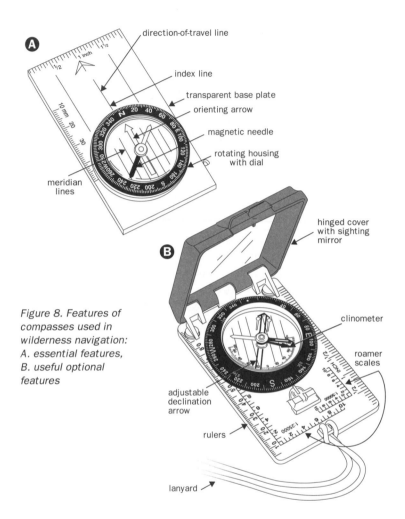

direction-of-travel line

index line

transparent base plate

orienting arrow

magnetic needle

rotating housing with dial

meridian lines

hinged cover with sighting mirror

clinometer

roamer scales

adjustable declination arrow

rulers

lanyard

Figure 8. Features of compasses used in wilderness navigation: A. essential features, B. useful optional features

lines; particularly useful when using a GPS receiver. If you get a compass without roamer scales, there are several other ways to identify your UTM position on topo maps (see chapter 6).

TIP: If you purchase a compass with roamer scales, be sure that it has the same scale(s) as your topographic map(s), for example, 1:24,000 for USGS topo maps in the United States, and 1:50,000 for metric maps in Canada and elsewhere.

Some compasses have an adjustable declination arrow but no mirror. These cost a little more than the basic compass of figure 8A but considerably less than the full-featured compass of figure 8B. They offer a good value for someone who prefers the adjustable declination arrow but does not want the added cost and/or weight of the mirror.

COMPASS SAFETY

Most compasses have a **lanyard**—a piece of cord a foot (30 cm) or a little longer for attaching the compass to your belt, jacket, or pack. It is not a good idea to put the lanyard around your neck; this can be an unsafe practice, particularly when doing any technical climbing, difficult scrambling, or when climbing over and under fallen logs, due to the possibility of strangulation. Furthermore, most lanyards are so short that the compass cannot be used effectively while it is around your neck anyway.

The baseplate compasses listed here are the ones we know about as we go to press. By the time the book hits the streets, some of these may be discontinued, while still others may appear. But this listing should at least give you an idea of the types of compasses that are available.

- **Full-featured** (see table 1): These top-of-the-line compasses have a declination adjustment and a mirror, and some have clinometers. Though more expensive than other compasses, these are best for wilderness navigation. We strongly recommend this type of compass.
- **With declination adjustment but no mirror** (see table 2): If you do not wish to get a full-featured compass, then we urge you to at least get one with adjustable declination, as listed in table 2. Note the designation *adjustable* declination; this is different from a *fixed (nonadjustable) declination scale,* which is a feature of some nonadjustable compasses.
- **With mirror but no declination adjustment** (see table 3): Some people buy this type of compass, mistakenly assuming that since it has a mirror it must also have adjustable declination; this is not true. We do not recommend this type. If you already have such a compass and do not wish to replace it, we

Table 1. Recommended Full-Featured Compasses

Brand & Model	Cost (in US dollars)	Weight (in ounces)	Roamer Scale	Magnifying Glass	Resolution (smallest division)	Gear-Driven Adjustment	Global (dip)	Clinometer	Luminous Points	Ruler(s)
Silva Ranger 515 CL*	52	2.4	✓	✓	2°	✓		✓	✓	✓
Silva Ranger CL Hi-Vis*	52	2.4	✓	✓	2°	✓		✓	✓	✓
Silva Type 15 Ranger*	97	2.4	✓		2°	✓		✓	✓	✓
Suunto MC-2 Pro*	56	2.6	✓	✓	2°	✓		✓	✓	✓
Suunto MC-2G Navigator*	84	2.6	✓	✓	2°	✓	✓	✓	✓	✓
Suunto MC-2D/L*	56	2.6	✓	✓	2°	✓		✓		✓
Suunto MC-2/360/G/D*	84	2.6	✓	✓	2°	✓	✓	✓	✓	✓
Brunton TruArc 15	50	3.2	✓	✓	1°		✓	✓	✓	✓
Brunton TruArc 20	60	3.6	✓	✓	1°		✓	✓		✓
K & R Dakar Touring	30	1.8			1°	✓				✓
K & R Sherpa BW2	73	2.5	✓	✓	2°	✓			✓	✓
K & R Lumo Tec	66	2			2°	✓		✓	✓	
K & R Alpin Sighting	85	2.5	✓	✓	2°	✓		✓	✓	✓

*Current favorites, according to The Mountaineers' navigation course information.

will show you how to adapt it for wilderness navigation use later in this chapter.

- **Minimal compasses** (see table 4): These meet all the basic requirements for wilderness travel but do not have features such as mirrors or declination corrections. We do not recommend any of these. However, if you already have such a compass and do not wish to replace it, we will show you how to adapt it for wilderness navigation use later in this chapter.

- **Unacceptable compasses:** Wrist and zipper-pull compasses, and those with scales marked in five-degree increments or without rectangular, transparent baseplates are unacceptable. Other unacceptable compasses are those found on smart phones, watches, and GPS devices, since they do not have transparent rectangular baseplates, and therefore cannot be used with maps.

If cost is not your primary factor, we strongly recommend any of the full-featured compasses if you can afford it. If minimum cost is your primary concern, any of the minimal compasses will work, though you will need to make a slight modification to correct for magnetic declination, which will be described later. If you can afford a better

Table 2. Recommended Compasses (without a sighting mirror)

Brand & Model	Cost (in US dollars)	Weight (in ounces)	Roamer Scale	Magnifying Glass	Resolution (smallest division)	Gear-Driven Adjustment	Global (dip)	Clinometer	Luminous Points	Ruler(s)
Silva Explorer Pro Hi-Vis*	31	1.4		✓	2°	✓		✓	✓	✓
Brunton 9020G	12	1.1			2°					✓
Brunton TruArc 3	13	1.1			2°	✓				✓
Brunton TruArc 5	20	1.8		✓	2°	✓				✓
Brunton TruArc 10	40	1.7	✓		1°	✓				✓
K & R Horizon	62	1.7	✓	✓	1°	✓		✓	✓	✓
Suunto M-3D/L*	35	1.6		✓	2°	✓			✓	✓
Suunto M-3 Global IN*	64	1.6		✓	2°	✓	✓	✓	✓	✓
Suunto M-3 Global CM*	34	1.6		✓	2°	✓	✓	✓	✓	✓
Suunto M-3 CM*	37	1.7		✓	2°	✓			✓	✓
Suunto M-3 IN*	37	1.7		✓	2°	✓			✓	✓

Note: All these compasses feature adjustable declination.
*Current favorites, according to The Mountaineers' navigation course information.

Table 3. Compasses without Adjustable Declination (not recommended)

Brand & Model	Cost (in US dollars)	Weight (in ounces)	Roamer Scale	Magnifying Glass	Resolution (smallest division)	Global (dip)	Clinometer	Luminous Points	Ruler(s)
Silva Trekker	25	1.5			2°				✓
Silva Guide 426 Graphite	23	0.9			2°				✓
Silva Guide 426 Orange	23	0.9			2°				✓
Silva Huntsman 426	23	0.9			2°				✓
Silva Guide 426	23	0.9			2°				✓
Suunto MCA-D IN	34	1.5			2°				✓
Suunto MCA-D CM	34	1.5			2°				✓
Suunto MCB Amphibian	30	1.3			2°				✓
Brunton Nexus Avalanche	26	1.2			2°	✓			✓
Brunton Nexus Pioneer	22	1.2			2°				✓
K & R M1 Sports Compass	43	2			2°			✓	

Note: These compasses are not recommended due to their lack of declination adjustment.

compass than the minimal but do not wish to spend enough to get a full-featured model, then we recommend getting a compass with a declination adjustment but without a mirror or clinometer. Of all the optional features, **the declination adjustment is the most useful.** We highly recommend this feature.

The Silva, Suunto, and K & R compasses listed in the tables have meridian lines in the transparent base, as shown in figure 8. Some of the Brunton models do not have meridian lines but can nevertheless be used successfully in wilderness navigation using slightly different methods. Other Brunton models have declination adjustment methods that differ from those used by other manufacturers. In order to simplify our explanation of compass use, we will defer the discussion of those Brunton models until chapter 7. The rest of the present chapter is therefore devoted to using compasses with meridian lines in the transparent base.

Table 4. Minimal Compasses (not recommended)

Brand & Model	Cost (in US dollars)	Weight (in ounces)	Roamer Scale	Magnifying Glass	Resolution (smallest division)	Global (dip)	Clinometer	Luminous Points	Ruler(s)
Silva Starter 1-2-3	13	0.9			2°				✓
Silva Polaris 177	16	1			2°				✓
Silva Polaris 177 Hi-Vis	16	1			2°				✓
Silva Explorer 203	22	1		✓	2°				✓
Silva Explorer III or Type 3	19	1		✓	2°				✓
Silva Polaris or Type 7	13	1			2°				✓
Suunto A-10 IN	22	2.2			2°				✓
Suunto A-10 CM	22	1.1			2°				✓
Suunto Arrow 20	67	1.1		✓	2°			✓	✓
Suunto Arrow 30	22	1.1		✓	2°			✓	✓
Suunto A-30 CM	22	1.1		✓	2°			✓	✓
Suunto A-30L IN	22	1.1		✓	2°			✓	✓
K & R K-1	13	1.1			2°				✓
K & R K-1L	35	1.4		✓	2°			✓	✓
Brunton 7DNL	13	1			2°				✓
Treknor Orienteer Deluxe	10	1.1			2°			✓	✓
Treknor Scout	10	1.4			2°				✓

Note: These compasses are not recommended because they lack sighting mirrors or adjustable declination.

SELECTING AND PURCHASING A COMPASS

Tables 1 through 4 contain the features and approximate costs for some of the most widely available compasses at the present time. For serious wilderness navigating, we recommend only those shown in tables 1 and 2. All of these have **adjustable declination**, a feature we consider nearly essential. Compasses that come with a small tool (usually connected to the lanyard) to make this adjustment, often referred to as a "gear-driven" adjustment, are recommended as the easiest to use and the most trouble-free.

The difference between the compasses in table 1 and those in table 2 is that those in table 1 have mirrors whereas those in table 2 do not. The primary **advantage of the mirror** is that most people can obtain more accurate compass readings with a mirrored compass. Furthermore, the mirror effectively doubles the length of the baseplate, thereby making it easier to use to measure and plot bearings on a map. (We will explain the use of the compass mirror later in this chapter.) Other purposes for the mirror include its possible use in emergency signaling, and to ensure complete coverage in the application of sunscreen to your face. If these features are not important to you, then you may consider a compass listed in table 2. Most of these are less expensive than those in table 1 but have many of the characteristics of the full-featured compasses other than the mirror.

The selection of compasses available at outdoor recreation and sporting goods stores is often limited. If you live near such stores, we suggest that you **try them first**, since you should be able to examine the compass carefully and try it out in the store before purchasing it. **Try the declination adjustment feature while in the store**, and ensure that it functions properly. We have heard complaints from some people who have purchased compasses with manufacturing defects and have had to return them. If the compass you want is not

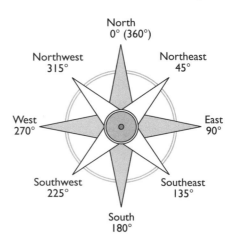

Figure 9. Cardinal and intermediate directions and corresponding bearings in degrees on the compass

available at a nearby store, then try an online website. Here, returning a defective unit is not as immediate as at a local store, but you will have a wider selection.

Before purchasing from an online source, be sure to check the company's return policy to ensure that you can easily return a defective compass. On some websites, you can view customers' reviews of particular compasses, to assess their strengths and weaknesses, and to learn of any problems others may have encountered with them.

BEARINGS

A **bearing** is the direction from one place to another, measured in degrees of angle with respect to an accepted reference line. This reference is the line to true north, also called a *meridian*.

The round dial of a compass is divided into 360°. The direction in degrees to each of the cardinal directions, going clockwise around the dial starting from the top, is north, 0° (also 360°); east, 90°; south, 180°; and west, 270° (see figure 9).

BEARING AND AZIMUTH

Technically, there is a subtle difference between these two terms, but in conventional modern usage they are essentially the same. A bearing has traditionally been defined as the angle between either north or south and another location, measured between zero and 90 degrees (such as S 45 W, meaning 45 degrees west of south). An azimuth, on the other hand, is the angle measured clockwise from north, from zero to 360 degrees (225 degrees in this same example). Many compass manufacturers today, however, define a bearing to be the same as the traditional definition of the azimuth. In this book, we treat the two as equivalent, and refer to them only by the term *bearing,* to be consistent with compass manufacturers. For example, some compasses have index lines that are marked "read bearing here."

The compass is used for two basic tasks regarding bearings:

1. *To take, or measure, bearings.* To take a bearing means to measure the direction from one point to another, either on a map or in the field.
2. *To plot, or follow, bearings.* To plot, or follow, a bearing means to

set a certain bearing on the compass and then to plot out, or to follow, where that bearing points, either on the map or in the field.

BEARINGS IN THE FIELD

All bearings in the field are based on where the magnetic needle points. For the sake of simplicity, we will first ignore the effects of magnetic declination, a subject that will be taken up in the next section. Let us imagine that we are in central Missouri, where the declination is negligible.

To take (measure) a bearing in the field: Hold the compass in front of you and

1. Point the direction-of-travel line at the object whose bearing you want to find.
2. Rotate the compass housing or bezel until the **pointed end of the orienting arrow is aligned with the north-seeking (usually red) end of the magnetic needle**. (This process is sometimes referred to as **boxing the needle** or "getting the dog in the doghouse.")
3. Read the bearing at the index line (see figure 10).

If the compass has no sighting mirror, hold it at or near arm's length and at or near waist level, with your arm straight at about a 45° angle from your body (see figure 11). This is a compromise between sighting with the compass at eye level (sighting on your objective along the edge of the compass, without

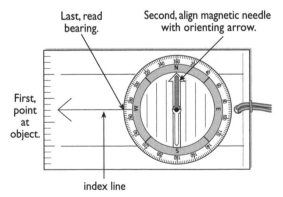

Last, read bearing.

Second, align magnetic needle with orienting arrow.

First, point at object.

index line

Figure 10. Taking a compass bearing in the field in an area with zero declination

Figure 11. Taking a bearing using a compass that does not have a mirror

Figure 12. Taking a bearing using a compass with a mirror

being able to see the compass needle or orienting arrow) or holding it straight down (being able to see the compass needle and arrow without parallax but losing sight of the objective).

With a sighting mirror, no such compromise is necessary. Fold the mirror back to about a 45° angle and hold the compass at eye level, with the sight pointing at the object (see figure 12). Observe the magnetic needle and the orienting arrow in the mirror as you rotate the housing to align the needle and the arrow (see figure 13). The centerline of the mirror should cross the pivot point of the magnetic needle. In either case, hold the compass

Figure 13. Close-up of taking a bearing using a compass with a mirror

level. Keep it away from metal objects, which can easily deflect the magnetic needle, giving you a false reading.

To follow (plot) a bearing in the field: Simply reverse the process you used to take a bearing.

1. Rotate the compass housing or bezel until you have set the desired bearing at the index line, say 270° (West).
2. Hold the compass level in front of you, at roughly arm's length and waist height. Turn your entire body (including your feet) until the north-seeking end of the magnetic needle is aligned with the pointed end of the orienting arrow (i.e., box the needle).
3. The direction-of-travel line is now pointing in whatever direction you have set at the index line, in this case west.

When following a bearing, it is best to find some object, such as a big rock or a unique-looking tree, that is in the same direction as the desired bearing. Then put the compass away and walk toward that object until you arrive at it, and repeat the process with another visible landmark. This is far better (safer and faster) than walking along, compass in hand, constantly observing the compass, rather than watching where you are going.

MAGNETIC DECLINATION

A compass needle is attracted to *magnetic north,* while most maps are printed with *true north*—the direction to the geographic north pole—at the top. This difference between the direction to true north and the direction to magnetic north, measured in degrees, is called **magnetic declination**. Most compasses will need a simple adjustment or modification to correct for declination.

Magnetic declination varies from place to place and over time. Always use the most current topographic map for your area. To find the amount and direction of declination for the map, look in the lower left corner on USGS topographic maps (see figure 6). If the map is more than a few years old, the declination may be somewhat out of date. The amount of declination changes over time, by as much as one degree every five years in some places in the United States. The map of the United States (except for Alaska) shown in figure 15 will give you a fairly good idea of the declination in your area. The map is for 2025 and is valid to within one degree for the time interval from 2020 to 2030. (See chapter 7 for more information on determining the correct present declination.) Figure 14 is a declination map for the state of Alaska, for the year 2025. It is valid to within one degree from 2022 to 2028.

In figure 15, you can see that the **line of zero declination** (called the *agonic line*) coincidentally runs through parts of Minnesota, Iowa, Missouri, Arkansas, and Louisiana at this time. Along this line, the magnetic needle points in the same direction as the geographic north pole (true north), so **no correction for declination is necessary**.

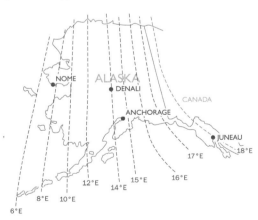

Figure 14. Magnetic declination in Alaska in 2025

In areas west of this line, the magnetic needle points somewhere to the east (to the right) of true north, so these areas are said to have *east declination*. It works just the opposite on the other side of the line of zero declination, such as on the East Coast of the United States

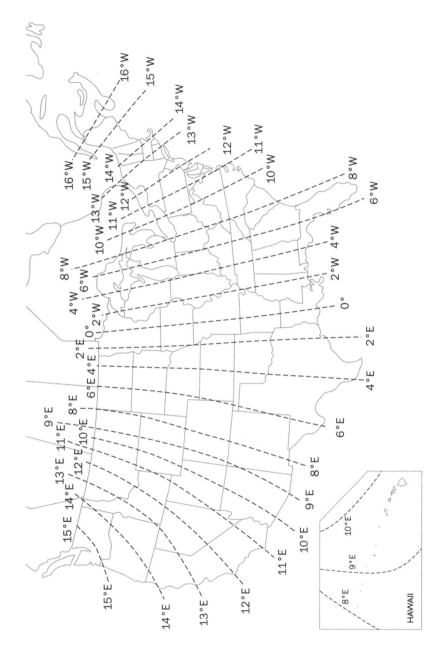

Figure 15. Magnetic declination in the contiguous United States and Hawaii in 2025

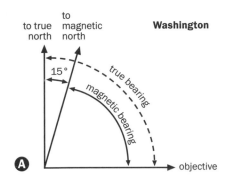

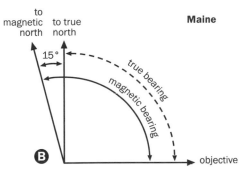

Figure 16. Magnetic and true bearings:
A. in Washington (east declination),
B. in Maine (west declination)

or Canada. Here, the magnetic needle points somewhere to the west (left) of true north, so these areas are said to have *west declination*.

Consider a wilderness traveler in western Washington state, with a declination of 15° east in 2025. The **true bearing** is a measurement of the angle between the line to true north and the line to the objective, as shown in figure 16A. The magnetic needle, however, is pulled toward magnetic north, not true north. So the compass measures the angle between the line to magnetic north and the line to the objective. This "magnetic bearing" is 15° less than the true bearing. To get the true bearing, you could add 15° to the magnetic bearing.

As in Washington state, travelers in all areas **west** of the zero declination line could **add the declination to the magnetic bearing** to get a true bearing. In central Colorado, for example, about 8° would be added. In western Utah, it is about 11°.

East of the zero declination line, the declination can be **subtracted from the magnetic bearing** to get the true bearing. In southern Maine, for example (see figure 16B), the magnetic bearing is about 15° greater than the true bearing. To get a true bearing, the traveler in Maine could subtract the declination of 15° from the magnetic bearing to obtain the true bearing.

This is all very simple in theory but can be confusing in practice, and the wilderness is no place for mental arithmetic that can have serious consequences. A more practical way to handle the minor complication of declination is to pay more for your compass and **get**

one with an adjustable declination arrow instead of a fixed orienting arrow. (These are the ones listed in tables 1 and 2 earlier.) By following the instructions supplied with the compass, you can easily set the declination arrow—usually by inserting a tiny screwdriver (often attached to the lanyard) into a small slot on the bezel and turning it until the declination arrow points at the correct number of degrees east or west of the index line. Then the bearing that you read at the index line will automatically be the true bearing, and concern about a declination error is one worry you can leave at home. Compasses with adjustable declination arrows are sometimes called "set and forget" compasses.

If you have a compass with adjustable declination and set it for a declination of 15° E, as for western Washington state, then, once properly adjusted, the pointed end of the declination arrow will point to 15°, as shown in figure 17. In Maine, with a declination of 15° W, the correctly adjusted declination arrow will point to 345° (15° less than 360°).

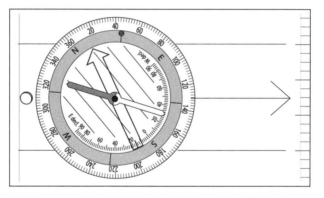

Figure 17. Compass with adjustable declination, set to 15° east declination, as for western Washington state in 2025

On compasses without adjustable declination arrows, you can achieve the same effect by sticking a thin strip of adhesive or masking tape to the bottom of the rotating housing or bezel to serve as a customized declination arrow. Trim the tape to a point, and apply it to the underside of the compass for the area where you will be traveling, as shown in figure 18.

In western Washington, your taped declination arrow must point at 15° east (clockwise) from the 360° point (marked *N* for north) on the rotating dial (figure 18A). In Maine, the declination arrow must point at 15° west (counterclockwise) from the 360° mark (figure 18B), or 345°.

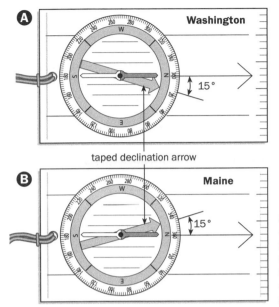

taped declination arrow

Figure 18. Compass declination corrections: A. for an area west of the zero-declination line, B. for an area east of the zero-declination line

Note that this taped declination arrow is located in exactly the same place as the adjustable declination arrow described above.

Some compasses have a nonadjustable **declination scale** numbered from 0° to 50° or more, both east and west. You can use this scale to locate the proper position for your taped declination arrow (such as 15° west rather than at 345°). Figure 19 illustrates a nonadjustable compass with such a taped declination arrow for a location in Labrador with a declination of 20 degrees west.

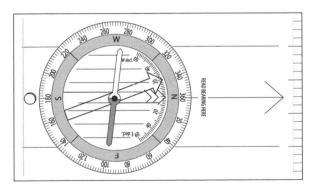

Figure 19. Taped declination arrow for a location in Labrador with declination 20° west

If you travel to an area with different declination, you will have to change the declination correction. If you have a compass with an adjustable declination arrow, a minor adjustment will allow you to set the compass for the new declination. If you have a taped declination arrow, you will have to peel the tape off and put a new arrow on, to correct for the new declination.

Once your compass is adjusted or modified for the proper declination, you can follow the same procedure to take and follow bearings as used in the earlier examples for Missouri. The only difference is that, from now on, you will **align the magnetic needle with the declination arrow** instead of with the orienting arrow.

> **TIP:** When using the magnetic needle in the field for taking and following bearings, always remember to **align the north-seeking (red) end** of the magnetic needle with the pointed end of the declination arrow to **box the needle.**

From here on we will assume that you are using a compass with a declination arrow—either an adjustable arrow or a taped arrow that you have added. For all bearings in the field, you will **align the needle with this declination arrow**. All compass bearings used from this point on are true bearings. We will not refer to magnetic bearings again, since we always automatically convert all bearings to true ones using one of the two techniques described above.

BACK BEARINGS

A **back bearing** (also called *back azimuth*) is the opposite direction of a bearing. This is also sometimes referred to as a *reciprocal* bearing. Back bearings are often useful when you are trying to follow a certain bearing, and you want to check to see if you are still on the bearing line by taking a back bearing on your starting point. If your original bearing is less than 180°, then you can find the back bearing by adding 180° to the original bearing. If your original bearing is greater than 180°, then you can find the back bearing by subtracting 180° from the original bearing. For example, if you are traveling at a bearing of 90°, then the back bearing is 270°. Once you reach your destination, following the back bearing of 270° should get you back to your starting point.

We previously mentioned that we do not recommend mental arithmetic in the wilderness, since it is too easy to make mistakes. A better way of working with a back bearing is to keep the original bearing at

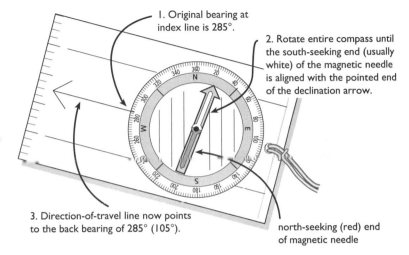

1. Original bearing at index line is 285°.

2. Rotate entire compass until the south-seeking end (usually white) of the magnetic needle is aligned with the pointed end of the declination arrow.

3. Direction-of-travel line now points to the back bearing of 285° (105°).

north-seeking (red) end of magnetic needle

Figure 20. Finding a back bearing using a compass

the index line, and rotate the compass until the **south-seeking end** (the white or black end) of the magnetic needle is aligned with the pointed end of the declination arrow, as shown in figure 20. The use of back bearings in wilderness navigation will be described in more detail in chapter 4.

BEARINGS ON A MAP

You can use your compass as a protractor, both to measure and to plot bearings on a map. Magnetic north and magnetic declination have nothing to do with these operations. Therefore, **ignore the magnetic needle** when measuring or plotting bearings on a map. (The only time you need to use the magnetic needle when working with the map is whenever you choose to orient the map to true north, which we will explain in chapter 3. But there is no need to orient the map to measure or plot bearings.)

To measure a bearing on a map (see figure 21):

1. Place the compass on the map with one long edge of the baseplate running between the two points of interest. To measure the bearing from point A to point B, make sure that the direction-of-travel line is pointing parallel to the direction **from A to B** (not the reverse).

2. Turn the rotating housing (bezel) until its set of meridian lines is parallel to the north–south lines of the map. Be sure that

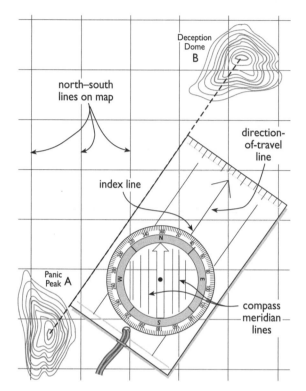

Figure 21. Measuring a bearing on a map with the compass as a protractor (magnetic needle omitted for clarity)

the N on the compass dial is toward the top of the map and that the S is toward the bottom. (If you put the N toward the bottom of the map, with the S toward the top, your reading will be 180° off.) For the utmost in accuracy, slide the compass along the bearing line so that one of its meridian lines is exactly on top of one of the north–south lines on the map.

3. Now read the number that is at the index line. This is the bearing from point A to point B.

Example: Suppose you are at the summit of Panic Peak, and you want to know which of the many peaks around you is Deception Dome. Your map shows both peaks (figure 21), so you can measure the bearing from point A, Panic Peak, to point B, Deception Dome. The result, as read at the index line, is 34°. (In this figure, we have purposely omitted the magnetic needle for the sake of clarity, and because it is not used here.) You can then hold the compass out in front of you and turn your entire body until you box the needle. The direction-of-travel line will then point toward Deception Dome and you can identify it.

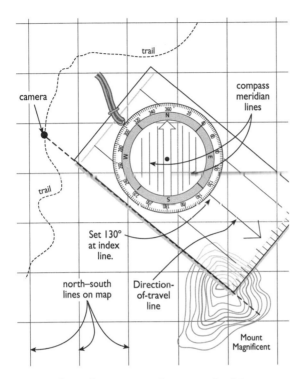

Figure 22.
Plotting a
bearing on a
map with the
compass as a
protractor
(magnetic
needle omitted
for clarity)

To plot a bearing on the map: In this case you are starting with a known bearing. And where does that bearing come from? From an actual landscape compass reading. Let us take a hypothetical example: Your friend returns from a backpacking trip, remorseful for having left a camera somewhere along the trail. While at a rest stop, your friend took a photo, and at the same spot had taken a bearing on Mount Magnificent and found it to be 130°. That is all you need to know. You are heading into that same area next weekend, so get out the Mount Magnificent quadrangle, and here is what you do (see figure 22):

1. First set the bearing of 130° at the compass index line. Place the compass on the map, one long edge of the baseplate touching the summit of Mount Magnificent.
2. Rotate the entire compass (not just the housing) until the meridian lines in the compass housing are parallel with the map's north–south lines, and make sure that the edge of the baseplate is still touching the summit. Again, make sure that the N on the compass dial is toward the top of the map.
3. Draw a line along the edge of the baseplate. Where this line crosses the trail is where your friend's camera is (or was).

When measuring or plotting bearings on a map, the map does not need to be in a horizontal position, such as lying down on the snow or dirt, on a stump, or in the mud. Instead, it can be vertical or in any other position. Its orientation doesn't matter, since you are just using the compass as a protractor.

In the forest, you can place the compass up against a tree to do the map and compass work. On a snowfield or glacier, with no trees, you can instead ask another member of the party to stand still while you steady the map against the person's pack or back. Or you can sit down on your pack, and do the map work in your lap or on your knee with your legs crossed.

PRACTICING WITH A COMPASS

Before you count on your compass skills in the wilderness, test them in an area near your home. The best place to practice is a place where you already know all the answers, such as at a street intersection where the roads run north–south and east–west.

- Take a bearing in a direction you know to be east. When you have pointed the direction-of-travel line at something that you know is east of you, such as along the edge of the street or sidewalk, and have boxed the needle, the number at the index line should be very close to 90°.
- Repeat for the other cardinal directions: south, west, and north (see figure 9). Then try all four again to see how repeatable the bearings are.
- Try to refine your technique to improve your accuracy. You may have to hold the compass higher or lower, or perhaps close one eye. Find out how accurate you can be. After some practice, you should consistently be able to get to within two degrees of the correct bearing. This is usually adequate. (If you cannot achieve this level of accuracy, or if you need better accuracy, you can get an optical sighting compass; see chapter 7).
- Then try the reverse process. Pretend you do not know which way is west. Set 270° (West) at the index line and hold the compass out in front of you as you turn your entire body (including your feet) until the needle is boxed. The direction-of-travel line should now point west. Does it?
- Repeat for the other three cardinal directions.

This set of exercises will help you to develop your skills related to and self-confidence around reading compasses and is also a way to check the accuracy of your compass. And if you make a mistake or two, well, no harm done.

You can practice measuring and plotting bearings on a map using the examples shown in figures 21 and 22. These figures are drawn with the correct angular proportions, so if you place your compass on the page you should get the same answers we get.

If you ever doubt the accuracy of your compass—perhaps because it has developed a small bubble or has given you a questionable reading in the field take it out to the street intersection again to test it. If the bearings you read are more than a few degrees away from the correct ones, consider replacing your compass. (Compass needles can sometimes become demagnetized or their magnetic orientation can even reverse, if the compass is stored in areas with strong electric or magnetic fields.)

Look for places to practice in the wilderness. A good place is any known location (such as a summit or a lakeshore) from which you can identify your exact position and can see identifiable landmarks. Take bearings on some of these and plot them on the map to see how close the result is to your actual location.

TIPS AND CAUTIONS FOR COMPASS USE

There is a big difference between using a compass for working with a map and using a compass for fieldwork. *In the field,* you must box the needle by aligning the pointed end of the declination arrow with the red end of the magnetic needle. When measuring and plotting bearings *on a map,* however, you ignore the compass needle. Just align the meridian lines in the compass housing with the north–south lines on the map, with the N of the compass dial toward north on the map. In both cases, the direction-of-travel line must point **from you to your objective**.

You may have heard that nearby metal can mess up a compass bearing. This is true. Ferrous objects such as iron and steel will deflect the magnetic needle and give **false readings**. Keep the compass away from belt buckles, ice axes, and other metal objects. Some wristwatches, particularly electronic ones, can also cause false readings if they are too close to the compass. Large electrical currents, such as those in nearby powerlines, can induce electromagnetic fields that can also disrupt compass bearings. If a compass reading does not make sense, see if nearby metal or electricity is sabotaging your bearing.

Keep your wits about you when pointing the direction-of-travel line and the declination arrow. If you point either of them backward—an easy thing to do—the reading will be **180° off**. If the bearing is north, the compass will say it is south. Remember that the north-seeking end of the magnetic needle must be aligned with the pointed end of the declination arrow and that the direction-of-travel line must point **from** you **to** your objective.

NAVIGATION TIP

Whenever you measure or plot bearings on a map, it is a good idea to first **guess at the answer**, based on your knowledge of the cardinal directions. Then if the bearing you carefully measure or plot is nowhere near your original guess, you may have made one of those **180° errors**.

For example, suppose you want to measure a bearing on a map, and this bearing is somewhere between northeast (45°) and east (90°). You might guess that it is 60° to 70° or so. Then suppose you measure the bearing as accurately as possible using your compass with the map. You line up one of the compass meridian lines exactly on top of one of the map's north–south lines, getting the bearing accurate to the nearest degree, and the number you read at your index line is 247°. Does this agree with your original guess? No! You must have made one of those 180° mistakes, and the correct answer is 67°.

When taking and following bearings in the field, you can also begin by making an intelligent guess at the result, then use the compass to get the exact answer. Before blindly following the compass, you can then ask yourself if the result from the compass agrees with your rough guess and common sense.

If in doubt, trust your compass. The compass, correctly used, is almost always right, while your contrary judgment may be clouded by fatigue, confusion, or hurry. If you get a nonsensical reading, check to see if perhaps you are making a 180° error. If not, and if no metal or electricity is nearby, verify the reading with other members of the party, using different compasses. If they get the same answer, trust your compass over hunches, blind guesses, and intuition.

CARRYING YOUR COMPASS

It is a good idea to carry your compass in a place that is readily accessible, so that you can easily and quickly check your compass **without taking off your pack**. Carrying your compass in a cargo pocket will accomplish this. If it is inconvenient to get to your compass, it is unlikely that you will use it when you should.

MAP AND COMPASS: A CHECKLIST

Do you have the hang of it? There are four essential compass operations that you must learn: taking and following bearings in the field, and measuring and plotting bearings on the map. Let us summarize these one last time. Check off each operation as you do it.

TO TAKE A BEARING IN THE FIELD

1. Hold the compass level, in front of you. Point the direction-of-travel line at the desired object.
2. Rotate the compass housing or bezel to align the pointed end of the declination arrow with the red end of the magnetic needle (box the needle).
3. Read the bearing at the index line.

TO FOLLOW A BEARING IN THE FIELD

1. Set the desired bearing at the index line.
2. Hold the compass level, in front of you. Turn your entire body, including your feet, until the red end of the magnetic needle is aligned with the pointed end of the declination arrow (box the needle).
3. Travel in the direction shown by the direction-of-travel line.

TO MEASURE A BEARING ON A MAP (see figure 21)

1. Place the compass on the map, with one long edge of the baseplate joining two points of interest. The direction-of-travel line points to your objective.
2. Rotate the housing to align the compass meridian lines with the north–south lines on the map, with N on the compass toward the top of the map.
3. Read the bearing at the index line.

TO PLOT A BEARING ON A MAP (see figure 22)

1. Set the desired bearing at the index line.
2. Place the compass on the map, with one long edge of the baseplate on the feature from which you wish to plot the bearing.
3. Turn the entire compass to align its meridian lines with the map's north–south lines, with N on the compass toward the top of the map. The edge of the baseplate is now on the bearing line.

Whenever you perform any of these operations, first guess at the answer, and perform the operation as accurately as you can. Then compare your answer to your original guess to ensure that you are not making a 180° error. Ensure that your answer makes sense to you.

AND FOR THE LAST TIME

- When taking and following bearings in the field, always align the pointed end of the declination arrow with the north-seeking (red) end of the magnetic needle (box the needle).
- Never use the magnetic needle or the declination arrow when measuring or plotting bearings on the map. Just make sure that the N on the compass dial is toward north on the map, not south, as a check to ensure that the compass meridian lines are not upside-down.

Once you master these four essential operations with the compass, you will have all the basic knowledge you need for map-and-compass orientation, navigation, and routefinding. The remainder of this book is based on these operations. If you thoroughly understand how to do them, you can proceed through the rest of the book with confidence, and you will easily understand everything that we explain.

If you are unsure of any of these four operations, we suggest that you stop now and **reread this chapter**. Study it carefully. Do the simple street-corner compass exercises we described for taking and following bearings. Measure and plot the bearings shown in figures 21 and 22. You must thoroughly understand each of these operations before proceeding with the rest of this book.

See chapter 7 for additional information on compasses and geomagnetism. You are particularly urged to read chapter 7 if you ever plan to travel to foreign lands on distant continents, where you may not know the declination or where the compass may be adversely affected by magnetic dip.

Once you thoroughly understand the basics, you are ready for orientation with map and compass.

CHAPTER SUMMARY

In this chapter you learned about baseplate compasses and how to deal with magnetic declination. You also learned about the four basic operations of compass use.

SKILLS CHECK

- List three features of a compass recommended for wilderness navigation.
- Briefly explain magnetic declination and its importance.
- List the four basic operations of compass use.

PRACTICE PROBLEMS *See the appendix for problem instructions.*

- Problems 17 and 24 involve measuring bearings on a map.
- Problem 18 involves plotting a bearing on a map.

Orientation with Map and Compass

Now that you have learned the fundamentals of map and compass use, you can put them to work to perform the process of **orientation**. This chapter will show you how to use map and compass techniques to determine exactly where you are on Earth's surface.

CHAPTER OBJECTIVES

- Master the science of orientation first by keeping track of your position through awareness and observation.
- Learn the meaning of point, line, and area position.
- Learn how to orient a map with your surroundings.
- Appreciate the usefulness of using the bearing of the slope.

Figuring out your exact location is usually relatively simple: just look around and compare what you see with what is on a map. Sometimes this is not accurate enough, or there is just nothing much nearby to identify on the map. The usual solution then is to get out the compass and to try for bearings on some landscape features, or to get out your GPS device. This is **orientation by instrument**. But before resorting to this, first study the map carefully to see if there are any topographic features—even subtle ones—that you can associate with the landscape around you. If you have been carefully observing your map and comparing it with the landscape, and keeping track of your location on the map (**continually orienting yourself**), as we suggested in chapter 1, you should always have a fairly good idea of where you are. Orientation by instrument should be reserved for those situations in which nothing else works, for compass practice, or for verifying your location after using other methods.

The goal of orientation is to determine that precise point on Earth's surface where you now stand. You can represent your position by a mere dot on the map. This is known as **point position**.

There are two lower levels of orientation. One is called *line position*: you know you are along a certain line on a map—such as a river, a trail, a ridge, a compass bearing, or a contour line—but you do not know where you are along that line.

The lowest level of orientation is *area position*: you know the general area you are in, but that is all. The objective of orientation is to determine your exact point position.

POINT POSITION

With point position known, you know exactly where you are, and you can use that knowledge to identify, on the map, any major feature that you can see in the landscape. You can also identify in the landscape any major visible feature that is shown on the map. Knowing your point position is an essential first step in navigation (see chapter 4).

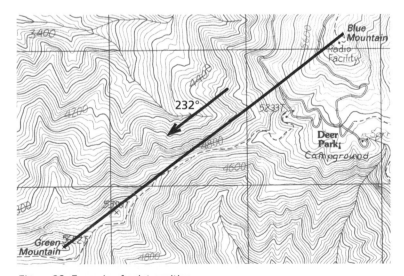

Figure 23. Example of point position

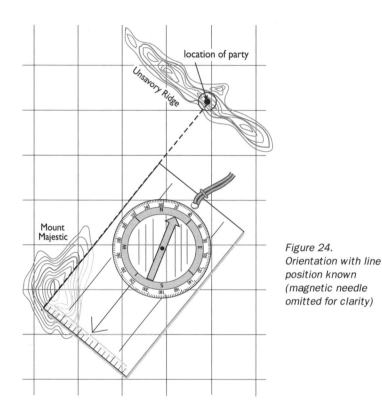

Figure 24.
Orientation with line
position known
(magnetic needle
omitted for clarity)

Suppose you have hiked to the summit of Blue Mountain (figure 23). You know your point position: the top of Blue Mountain. You see an unknown peak and want to know what it is. You take a compass bearing on it and get 232°. You plot 232° from Blue Mountain on your map, and the plotted line passes through Green Mountain. The unknown peak is Green Mountain. However, if you start by wanting to determine which of the many peaks around you is Green Mountain, you must do the map work first. You measure the bearing on the map from where you are, Blue Mountain, to Green Mountain, and get 232°. Keeping the 232° at the index line, the entire compass is turned until the needle is boxed. The direction-of-travel line then points toward Green Mountain.

LINE POSITION

With line position known, the goal is to determine point position. If you know that you are on a trail, a ridge, or some other easily identifiable *line,* you need only one more trustworthy piece of information to get your point position.

Example: Suppose a party of scramblers is on Unsavory Ridge (figure 24), but they do not know exactly where they are on the ridge. In the distance is Mount Majestic. A bearing on it indicates 218°. They plot 218° from Mount Majestic on the map, and run this line back toward Unsavory Ridge. Where it intersects the ridge is where the scramblers are.

AREA POSITION

If you only know your general area, you need at least two trustworthy pieces of information to determine your point position.

Example: Suppose some snowshoers know they are in the general area of Fantastic Crags (figure 25), their area position. They want to determine line position and then, from that, point position. They may be able to use bearings on two known, recognizable features. They take

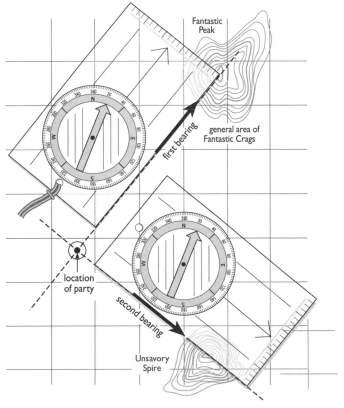

Figure 25. Orientation with area position known (magnetic needle omitted for clarity)

a bearing on Fantastic Peak and get a reading of 38°. They plot a line on the map, along the baseplate and through Fantastic Peak, at 38°. They know they must be somewhere on or near that bearing line, so they now have line position. They can also see Unsavory Spire. A bearing on the spire shows 130°. They plot this line on the map, through Unsavory Spire, and draw a line along the baseplate. The two bearing lines intersect, and that is their location—or approximately so.

Whenever you take a bearing in the field or plot a bearing on a map, it is inevitable that minor errors will creep in to create larger errors in the estimate of your position. It is very easy to make an error of 3° in taking a bearing, and another 2° in plotting that bearing, unless you are extremely careful. For every 5° of error, your position will be in error by about 460 feet in every mile (about 90 meters in every kilometer). If you take and plot a bearing on a landmark 3 miles (5 km) away, and make a 5° error, the plotted line could be about 1400 feet (430 m) away from the correct position. Therefore, be sure that your **conclusions agree with common sense**. If you take and plot bearings from two peaks and find that the two lines intersect in the middle of a river, but you are standing on a high point of land, something is wrong. Try again. Try to take a more accurate bearing, and plot it more carefully. If bearing lines intersect at a map location with no similarity to the terrain, you may have errors in your bearings. Or there might be some magnetic anomaly in the rocks, or you might have an inaccurate map. And who knows? Maybe those peaks are not really the peaks you think they are.

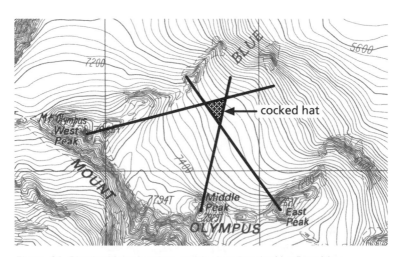

Figure 26. Plotting three bearings results in a "cocked hat" position.

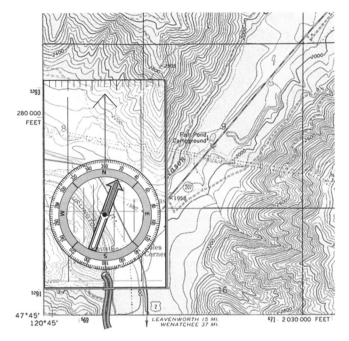

Figure 27. Using a compass to orient a map in an area with 20 degrees east declination

Make sure that the two bearings are not from approximately the same direction, since this can compound any error. **The closer an angle of intersection is to 90°, the more accurate** the point position will be.

The technique of taking and plotting bearings from landmarks is more accurate if you can see **three landmarks** and plot three bearings. The result will be a small triangle (called a "cocked hat," see figure 26). Your position is most likely within this triangle.

ORIENTING A MAP

During a wilderness excursion it sometimes helps to hold the map in a traditional manner so that north on the map is pointed in the actual direction of true north. This is known as **orienting the map**, a good way to obtain a better feel of the relationship between the map and the countryside.

One way to orient a map is **by inspection**: simply look at the terrain and compare it to the map. Then hold the map level and turn it until the map is lined up with the terrain.

Often, this technique will not work because you cannot see any identifiable features around you. In this case, you can orient your map **using your compass**. Set 360° (North) at the index line of the compass and place your compass on the map. Put one long edge of the baseplate along the left or right edge of the map as shown in figure 27, with the N of the compass dial pointing to the direction of north on the map. Then hold the map level and turn the map and compass together until the needle is boxed. The map is now oriented to the scene around you. (Map orientation can give you a general feel for the area but cannot replace the more precise methods of orientation that we covered in the preceding paragraphs.)

DIRECTION AND BEARING OF THE SLOPE

You can often find your position by using the **direction of the slope**, which was first described in chapter 1 using general directions such as east or southwest. This technique can be refined by using the more precise **bearing of the slope**. For example, suppose you are hiking along the trail near Maiden Peak (figure 28) and want to find your point position. You take a bearing on Maiden Peak and get 242°. You plot this bearing and find that it crosses the trail in two places, A and B. Where are you? Points A and B are both on a ridge, but at point A the slope falls off to the east, while at point B it falls off to the north. Suppose you take your compass and point it in the direction of the slope. You find that the actual slope falls off to the north. That tells you that you are at point B, not point A.

Sometimes the situation is a little more subtle, so we need more accuracy with this approach. In this case, we refer to the bearing of the slope rather than merely its general direction. Imagine that another party is also on the Maiden Peak trail and wants to find its position. Some party members take a bearing on Maiden Peak and get 42°. They plot this line, as shown in figure 28, and they see that the bearing line crosses the trail in three places. Where are they, point C, D, or E? A quick compass bearing shows that the slope falls off roughly to the southeast, so point D is ruled out, since at that point the map clearly shows the slope to fall off to the east. That narrows it down to either point C or point E. A party member faces downhill and takes a more careful bearing in the direction of the fall line. Suppose the bearing is 140°. One long edge of the compass is then placed on the map at

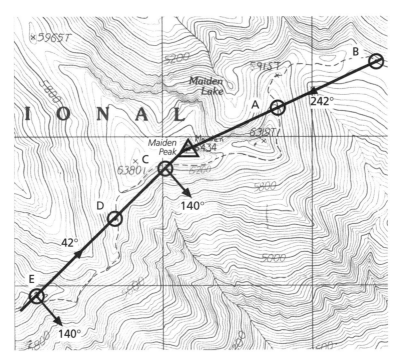

Figure 28. Using the bearing of a slope to find your position

point C, and the entire compass is rotated until the meridian lines in the compass housing are parallel with the north–south lines on the map, with the N on the compass dial toward the top of the map. The edge of the baseplate should then point in a direction perpendicular to the contour lines at point C. However, you can see that the bearing of 140° is *not* perpendicular to the contour lines at point C. So instead the same process can be repeated for point E. This time, the bearing line is nearly perpendicular to the contour lines, at least for the first 200 feet down from point E. From this, the party concludes that it is at point E.

A REMINDER

At the beginning of this chapter we said that orientation by instrument should be reserved for those situations in which nothing else works. The best method of orientation is to **use your map and your continual observations of topography** to keep track of where you are. Presumably, at the beginning of your trek you know where you are and can identify that position on the map. If you then follow your progress on the map, noting each topographic or other feature that you pass along the way, then at any time you should know your position with a great amount of certainty. It is essential to know the technical methods of map and compass orientation (and possibly GPS; see chapter 9), but there is still **no substitute for continually keeping track of your position using the map (orientation)**.

SITUATIONAL AWARENESS

When you ignore cues from the terrain, your "situational awareness" is diminished, which directly affects your safety. Fight this tendency with several techniques. Start by observing your surroundings and updating your mental map of the landscape. Correlate your surroundings with the physical map. Study myriad details, including slope, sun position, ridges, and terrain features, and confirm them using your altimeter and compass. Then decide on your next steps. Maintain your heightened sense of situational awareness by repeating this observe-orient-decide-act cycle while you move through the landscape.

Maintaining situational awareness is not just a topic of navigation but of safety in general: What is happening with the weather? What is the condition of the party? How many hours of daylight remain? Maintaining a high level of situational awareness can help keep you on course and safe.

CHAPTER SUMMARY

In this chapter you learned about the importance of orientation by keeping track of your position through awareness and observation; the difference between point, line, and area position; and how to orient a map with your surroundings.

SKILLS CHECK

- List two examples each of point, line, and area position.
- Describe the technique for measuring the bearing of a slope.

PRACTICE PROBLEMS *See the appendix for problem instructions.*

- Problems 8, 16, 19, 20, 23, 25, and 26 provide opportunities for you to practice the principles of orientation.

Chapter
4

Navigation with Map and Compass

Now that you have learned the fundamentals of orientation, you can determine exactly where you are. You can then determine the direction to travel to get to your desired destination: the process of navigation. This chapter will explain a variety of methods to do so.

CHAPTER OBJECTIVES

- Learn the principles of terrain navigation by following natural topographic features.
- Learn how to find the route to a distant objective using map and compass.
- Follow a route using compass alone.
- Make use of *aiming off* (an intentional offset).
- Cope with the special problem of the parallel path.
- Learn techniques for navigating around an obstruction.
- Know the importance of maintaining awareness of where you are and where you are headed.

Getting from here to there is usually just a matter of keeping an eye on the landscape and watching where you are going, helped by an occasional glance at the map. However, if you cannot see your objective in the field, you can measure the bearing on the map, then take compass in hand and follow the direction-of-travel line as it guides you to the goal. This is **navigation by instrument**. It is a technique that will work if you are able to follow a straight-line route, something often impossible in wilderness terrain. For this reason, it is best to **first try to follow trails or topographic features** in wilderness navigation, and reserve navigation by instrument for those situations where the topography lacks sufficient features to be of any help to you.

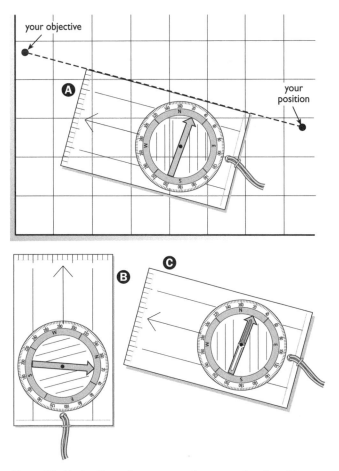

Figure 29. Navigation using a map and compass (on A and B, magnetic needle omitted for clarity): A. measuring the bearing on the map from your position to your destination, B. reading the bearing at the index line (leave the compass set), C. following the bearing

Navigation by instrument is sometimes the only practical method for finding a crucial pass, base camp, or other goal. It also serves as a supplement to other methods, such as following topographic features, and it can help to verify that you are on the right track. Again, use common sense and challenge a compass reading that defies reason. (Is your declination arrow or direction-of-travel line pointing the wrong way, sending you 180° off course?)

MAP AND COMPASS NAVIGATION

The most common situation requiring instrument navigation comes when the route is unclear because the topography is featureless or because landmarks are obscured by forest or fog. You know exactly where you are and exactly where you want to go, and you can identify both your present position and your destination on the map. In this case, simply measure the bearing from your present position to your objective on the map, and then follow that bearing to your objective.

Example: Suppose you measure a bearing of 285° on the map (figure 29A). Note that the north–south lines in the compass housing are parallel with the north–south lines on the map, with the N on the compass dial aligned with the top of the map. Read this bearing at the index line and leave it set there (figure 29B). Then hold your compass out in front of you as you rotate your body until you have boxed the needle. The direction-of-travel line now points to your objective (figure 29C). Start walking.

COMPASS ALONE

Navigators of air and ocean often travel by instrument alone; you can too. For example, suppose you are scrambling toward a ridgetop

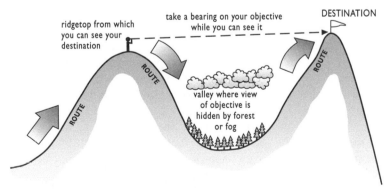

Figure 30. Following a compass bearing when the view of the objective is obscured by forest or fog

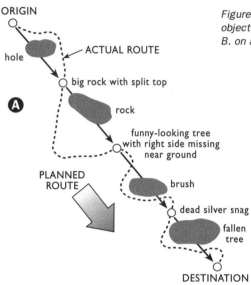

ORIGIN

hole

ACTUAL ROUTE

big rock with split top

A

rock

funny-looking tree
with right side missing
near ground

PLANNED
ROUTE

brush

dead silver snag

fallen
tree

DESTINATION

*Figure 31. Use of intermediate
objectives: A. in the forest,
B. on a glacier*

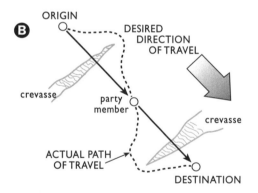

ORIGIN

B

DESIRED
DIRECTION
OF TRAVEL

crevasse

party
member

crevasse

ACTUAL PATH
OF TRAVEL

DESTINATION

and clouds begin to obscure your view. Just take a quick compass bearing on the destination before it disappears from view, then follow that bearing, compass in hand if you wish. You do not even have to note the numerical bearing; just box the needle and keep it boxed as you proceed to your objective. Likewise, if you are heading into a valley where fog or forest will hide your destination, take a bearing on that goal before you drop into the valley, and then follow that bearing after you lose sight of the objective (figure 30). This method becomes more reliable if several people travel together, checking each other's work by taking occasional back bearings on each other.

USING INTERMEDIATE OBJECTIVES

A handy technique is available for those frustrating times when you try to travel exactly along a compass bearing but are frequently diverted by obstructions such as cliffs, dense brush, or crevasses. Try the technique of **intermediate objectives**. If in a forest, sight past the obstruction to a tree or rock or other object that is exactly on the bearing line to the principal objective (figure 31A). Then you are free to travel over to the tree or rock by whatever route is easiest. When you get to the intermediate objective, you can be confident that you are still on the correct route. This technique is useful even when there is no obstruction. Moving from one intermediate objective to another means you can put the compass away for those stretches, rather than having to hold it continually in your hand and check it every few steps.

Sometimes on snow or glaciers, in fog, or in a forest where all the trees look the same, there may be no natural intermediate objectives. In this case, another member of the party can serve as the target (figure 31B). Send that person out to near the limit of visibility or past the obstruction. Wave that person left or right until he or she is directly on the bearing line. That person can improve the accuracy of the route by taking a back bearing on you.

THE INTENTIONAL OFFSET ("AIMING OFF")

Now imagine that your party is almost back to the car after a scramble. You follow a compass bearing

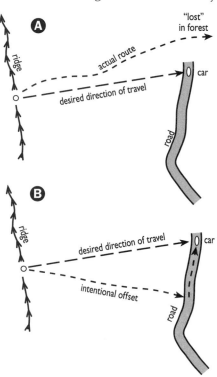

Figure 32. Navigating to a specific point on a line: A. Inevitable minor errors can sometimes have disastrous consequences. B. To avoid such problems, follow a course with an intentional offset.

to the logging road, but you cannot see the car because you are off route by a few degrees. You have to guess which way to go. It is a bad ending to the trip if the car is to the right and you go left. It will be even worse if the car is parked at the end of the road, and a routefinding error takes the party beyond that point and on and on through the woods (figure 32A). The **intentional offset** (also called "**aiming off**") was invented for this situation (figure 32B). Just travel in a direction that is intentionally offset by 20° to 30° to the right or the left of wherever you want to be. When you hit the road, there will be no doubt about which way to turn.

THE PARALLEL PATH

One of the most vexing navigational problems can be the situation encountered when traveling in a direction that parallels the direction of a road, trail, or other feature to which you must return in order to get back home. Such a situation is illustrated in figure 33. A party drives along a fairly straight road to its end, parks the car, and hikes to the objective in a direction exactly parallel to the road. Both the road and the objective are clearly visible on the map, so once at the objective the party can follow the back bearing to the road end. When following this bearing back, however, it might not be possible to stay exactly on route, due to irregularities in the topography. Consequently, when the party nears the car, it may have missed the end of the road and ended up in the woods to either the right or the left of the road.

With a little forethought, they could have avoided this situation by using a variation of the aiming-off technique. They could have purposely taken a route 20° to 30° to the left or the right of the correct path, to a point safely past the end of the road. Once sure they were past this point, they could then turn sharply toward the road, and they would soon intersect it. A short hike up the road

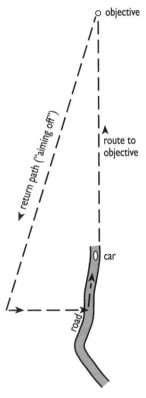

Figure 33. Example of traveling on a path parallel to a road, trail, or other line position

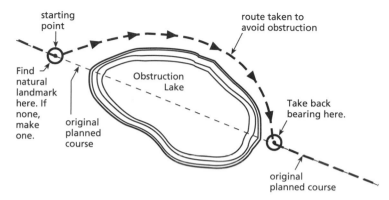

Figure 34. Navigating around an obstruction when you can see across it once you are past it

would then lead them back to the car. The overall trip would be longer than if they had taken a direct path, but the latter might have caused them to miss the road entirely.

NAVIGATING AROUND AN OBSTRUCTION

Sometimes you may try to follow a constant bearing to get to your objective but find that the route is blocked by an obstruction such as a lake or a cliff. There may be an easy way to get around the obstruction, but doing so forces you off your intended bearing. What do you do to stay on the correct bearing?

If the obstruction is a lake or swamp, you may be able to see across it back to your starting point after you have traveled past it (figure 34). In this case, try to find some large, **easily visible object on your bearing line** before you start traveling past the obstruction. If that point is a nondescript location with no identifiable landmark, you can mark this spot by building a pile of fallen logs or some other temporary landmark that you will be able to see from the other side of the obstruction. (See "Mark the Route If Necessary" in chapter 5.) Once you know that you have an identifiable object or marker along your bearing line, you can walk around the obstruction using whatever route is easiest. Once past the obstruction, take a **back bearing** on your starting point. If this does not match the bearing of your intended direction of travel, then continue around the obstruction until your back bearing on the starting point does match your intended direction of travel.

If the obstruction is a cliff, a hill, or some other feature that prevents you from seeing your starting point once you have passed the

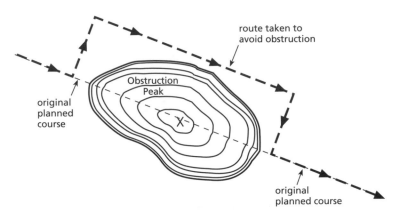

Figure 35. Navigating around an obstruction when the view across it is blocked

obstruction, then you may have to use a different technique, as shown in figure 35. In this case, you can travel a paced distance at 90° to the original course, then go past the blockage on a bearing parallel to the original course, and finally return to the original course by another 90° course change paced the same distance as the earlier one but in the opposite direction. (The course change need not be 90°. It could be 45° or some other direction, as long as it is easily possible to return to the original direction of travel.)

ALWAYS KEEP THE RETURN ROUTE IN MIND

No party should ever wander off on what may appear to be an obvious route without taking note of the direction they are heading and planning how they will return.

Example: Suppose that a party follows a trail to a camp in the forest (figure 36). After eating dinner, they decide to hike off-trail to a clearly visible pass to see the view. After enjoying a memorable sunset at the pass, they turn around to return to camp. At that point it occurs to them that they cannot see their camp, do not know the direction to it, and will shortly be running out of daylight. Is this a problem? It all depends on the preparations they made on the hike to the pass.

If they had merely headed up to the pass without any thought of how they would get back, they might be in trouble. If, on the other hand, they had taken a compass bearing from their camp to the pass when they started their trek, then once at the pass they could simply follow a back bearing from the pass to return to their camp in the forest. They could have also used route-marking materials to mark the spot where they emerged from the forest. (If you do this, be sure to remove the marker once you no longer need it. Good wilderness travelers practice Leave-No-Trace principles: take only pictures, leave only footprints.) These simple measures could turn a potentially serious problem into a routine after-dinner stroll.

A REMINDER

At the start of this chapter we recommended using topographic features whenever possible in off-trail navigation, and reserving the use of navigation by instrument only for those situations in which the topography lacks sufficient features. Now, after describing eight different techniques used in off-trail navigation, we are concerned that we may have distracted you from the original point, so we will repeat it: Wherever possible, **navigate by using trails and natural topographic features**, while keeping track of your position on the map. Reserve the use of navigation by instrument for those situations where there is no alternative.

If you have thoroughly mastered the sciences of orientation and navigation, and keep these principles in mind as you navigate toward your objective and back, it is unlikely that you will ever get lost.

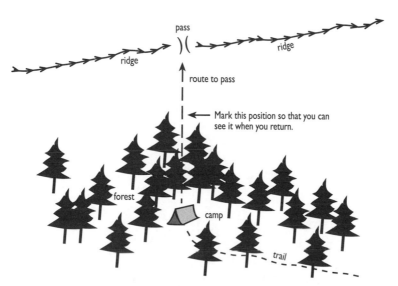

Figure 36. Example of traveling via obvious route to a destination from which the return trip will not be obvious

CHAPTER SUMMARY

In this chapter you learned about navigation by following trails and natural topographic features as well as by using map and compass. You also learned about the usefulness of the intentional offset and other techniques. We have also reinforced the importance of maintaining map awareness of where you are at all times.

SKILLS CHECK

- What is the best way to navigate to your objective?
- What are the three steps for navigation by map and compass? Briefly describe taking a bearing from a map and following that bearing in the field.
- Explain two uses for utilizing an intentional bearing offset.
- How can you stay on course if you need to navigate around an obstruction?

PRACTICE PROBLEMS *See the appendix for problem instructions.*

- Problems 22 and 28 provide opportunities for you to practice the principles of navigation.

Lost!

Note: If you turned to this chapter first, after seeing its title in the table of contents, please **go back** to the beginning of the book and read chapters 1 through 4 before reading this chapter. The focus of this chapter is to prevent you from getting lost, which requires a thorough knowledge of map, compass, orientation, and navigation.

CHAPTER OBJECTIVES

- Know how to avoid getting lost by identifying baselines, handrails, and potential routefinding problems.
- Learn steps you can take before and during the trip to ensure that you stay on track and do not get lost.
- Know what to do if you ever *do* get lost.

The primary focus of this book is to give you the necessary skills and knowledge to **avoid getting lost** in the first place. Later in this chapter we will give you some suggestions concerning what to do if you ever *do* get lost. But you should always know where you are if you:

- have carefully read and absorbed the preceding four chapters;
- carry a topographic map of the area and a good compass;
- have adequately practiced map reading, compass use, orientation, and navigation; and

- maintain orientation at all times, by keeping track of your position on the map throughout your trip.

If so, you are not lost, and this entire subject may be only of academic interest to you. In addition to the information provided in the first four chapters, the information given in this chapter may go a long way toward preventing you from ever getting lost in the first place.

HOW TO AVOID GETTING LOST

You can minimize your likelihood of getting lost with adequate planning before you ever leave home and by taking certain precautions during the trip to your destination and on the return from it.

Before the Trip

Most wilderness orientation, navigation, and routefinding is done by simply looking at your surroundings and comparing them to the map. This process is often aided by making some navigational preparations before the trip, like identifying handrails, baselines, and possible routefinding problems.

A **handrail** is a linear feature on the map that you can follow, or it may be a feature that parallels the direction in which you are heading. The handrail should be within frequent sight or sound (such as a noisy babbling brook) of the route, so it can serve as an aid in navigation. Features that you can use as handrails during a trip include:

- Roads
- Trails
- Railroad tracks
- Powerlines
- Fences
- Cliff bands
- Borders of fields and meadows
- Ridges
- Valleys
- Lakeshores
- Edges of marshes
- Rivers and streams

A **baseline** is a long, unmistakable line that always lies in the same direction from you, no matter where you are during the trip. Pick out a baseline on the map during trip planning. It does not have to be something you can see during the trip. You just have to know that it is there, in a consistent direction from you. A baseline (sometimes called a *catch line*) can be:

- A road
- An obvious trail
- The shore of a large lake
- A river or creek
- A powerline
- Any other feature that is at least as long as your trip area

If the shore of a large distant lake always lies west of the area you will be in, you can be sure that heading west at any time will eventually get you to this identifiable landmark. Heading toward this baseline may not be the fastest way to travel back home from your destination, but it may save you from being truly lost.

Before the trip, it is wise to prepare a **route plan**: a well-thought-out description of how you will find your way to your destination and back, including handrails, baselines, trails, topographic features you will be following, and other aspects of your proposed wilderness trek. It is also a good idea to highlight the entire trip on a topographic map.

1. **Identify handrails, baselines, and other features** that you will be following on the way to your objective. Part of this plan is to recognize potential routefinding problems. For example, if the route traverses a large, featureless area, you may need **route-marking materials**, particularly if the weather outlook is marginal. Be sure to carry such materials if your route plan indicates a possible need for them.
2. **Make a note of any escape routes** that can be used in case of sudden bad weather, injury, or other setbacks.
3. If off-trail travel is involved, **measure compass bearings at home** before the trip and write them down in a notebook or note them on the map. It is certainly possible to measure map bearings at any point in the trip, but it is easier and sometimes more accurate at home on a desk or table, and it might save you time in an emergency.

BASELINE NAVIGATION EXAMPLE

A party once began a long scramble but was turned around due to bad weather. They started to drive home but had a flat tire on the way. While two party members changed the tire, the other passengers noticed some delicious edible mushrooms alongside the road. A little exploration revealed that the deeper into the woods they ventured, the more numerous and luscious the mushrooms became. They told the others, and after the tire was changed they all decided to dump their pack contents in the trunk of the car and head out into the woods to fill their packs with mushrooms.

After an hour or so, sunset approached and their packs were filled, but the party had not paid any attention to where they had been going, had taken no compass bearings, and had not followed any recognizable topographic features, since the terrain was forested, flat, and featureless. Was this a problem? Not really. They knew that the road they were traveling ran almost true north–south (figure 37). They also knew that they had not crossed the road, so they had to be on the east side of the road. Some party members had their compasses in their pockets, so they could easily set their compasses on a course due west. A short ramble in the woods brought them back to the road, and they could see their car. This is a classic example of baseline navigation.

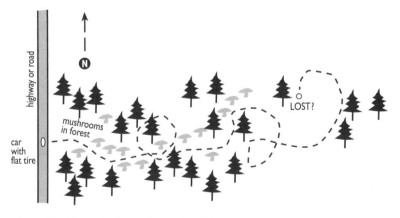

Figure 37. Example of baseline navigation

4. **Write down and discuss your route plan** with other members of the party, so the party is not solely dependent on one person for all route decisions. You might consider requiring all party members (or at least children or inexperienced persons) to carry whistles.

5. Be sure to **tell a responsible person where you are going,** what route you are taking, and when you plan on returning. This will not prevent you from getting lost. But if you do run into trouble, the authorities will know to look for you, and where to look. **This one bit of preparation could save your life.** (It could be as easy as texting a friend while you are still within cell phone range, such as "Day trip to Lk 22 with Dad and Ron. Silver Ford Fusion WA license SHWK12. Will text u when we return." It could be more elaborate, such as marking a copy of a topo map with your planned route and emailing it to your responsible person, along with the trip schedule.)

> **TIP:** Be sure that you have the most recent road, trail, and avalanche conditions and a weather forecast for your trip. Check online or at the local ranger station for the latest information.

Always make sure that every member of the party carries adequate food, clothing, and other supplies (see "Survival," below). In the event of any emergency, each person should have:

- enough food and clothing to survive several days, if necessary, while waiting for search and rescue personnel to arrive; and
- a map of the area and a compass, in case anyone becomes separated from the rest of the group.

Every wilderness excursion, no matter how simple, should have an agreed-upon **turnaround time**. If you have not reached your objective by this time, then you must turn around to reach the trailhead or other starting point with adequate daylight remaining. (Additional information on turnaround time for various situations is given in chapter 10 of this book.)

During the Trip

Get off on the right foot by making sure that everyone understands the route and the route plan.

- Gather the party around a map, and take time to discuss the route and to make contingency plans in case the party becomes separated.
- Point out on the map where you are, and associate your surroundings with the piece of paper in front of you. This is a good time for everyone to make a mental note of the main features—such as forests, streams, ridges, valleys, mountain peaks, and trails—they will see during the trip.

Along the way, everyone needs to continue **associating the terrain with the map**. Ignorance of the territory is definitely not bliss for any daydreaming person who becomes separated from the party. Whenever a new landmark appears, connect it with the map. At every chance—at a pass, in a clearing, or through a break in the clouds—update your fix on the group's exact position. Keeping track of your progress on the map makes it easy to plan each succeeding leg of the trip. It may also turn you into an expert map reader because you will quickly learn what a specific valley or ridge looks like compared to its representation on the map.

Use handrails wherever possible. When the inevitable moment comes for you to leave the security of your handrail, such as a trail, make a mental note of the fact that you are leaving it, and ask yourself what you will be following instead—some topographic feature, a contour line, a compass bearing, or anything else you can count on. You should not merely press onward without a clear idea of where you are headed or how to get back.

Keep the party together, except perhaps on well-traveled, obvious trails. Allow party members to travel at their own pace, but agree ahead of time to stop and regroup at certain bridges, stream crossings, and—most importantly—trail junctions. Even then do not let the group get too spread out, and agree ahead of time on places to stop and wait for everyone to catch up. If the group includes children or inexperienced persons, keep them in sight at all times.

ASSIGN A SWEEP

Assign a responsible, experienced person to be the **rear guard**, or "sweep," to ensure that no straggler will be left behind or lost.

STAYING ORIENTED EN ROUTE

You can take several steps to stay oriented while on a wilderness trip.

Look Ahead to the Return Trip

The route always often looks different on the way back. Avoid surprises and confusion by

- glancing over your shoulder often and especially at route junctions on the way in to see what the route should look like on the return.
- jotting down times, elevations, landmarks, and so on in a small notebook, or even in the margin of your map. A few cryptic words, such as "7600, hit ridge," can save you a lot of grief on the return. It will remind you that when the party has dropped to 7600 feet, it is time to leave the ridge and start down to your starting point.

Think

Your brain is your most important navigational tool, a fact often overlooked amid our reliance on compasses, altimeters, GPS receivers, and other gadgets. As the party heads toward its destination, **keep asking yourself questions:**

- How will we recognize this important spot on our return?
- What would we do if the trip leader became unconscious? (Are we all relying on one person?)
- Could I find my way back alone if I had to?
- Would we be able to find our way back in a whiteout or if snow covered our tracks?
- Should we be marking the route right now?
- How are we doing with regard to the previously agreed-upon turnaround time?

Ask the questions as you go, and act on your answers. Make decisions for you and your team before weather, route, time, and terrain make the decisions for you.

Mark the Route If Necessary

There are times when it may be best to **mark the route** going in so you can find it again on the way out. This situation can occur when:

Figure 38. Rock cairn

- the route passes over snowfields or glaciers during changeable weather,
- in heavy forest, or
- when fog threatens to hide landmarks.

On snow, climbers use thin bamboo *wands* with little flags to mark the path (see "Wands" in chapter 10).

In wooded areas, you can create temporary markers out of natural materials such as downed branches or logs. For example, at a trail junction, you can arrange branches in the shape of an arrow to point the way to the correct route, or in the shape of an "X" across the trail to indicate the incorrect route.

In the forest, plastic surveyor's tape is sometimes tied to branches to show the route, but we strongly discourage its use due to its permanence, since we always endeavor to leave no trace.

From an ecological standpoint, toilet paper is the best marker, because it will disintegrate during the next rainfall. Use a small streamer of toilet paper if you are assured of good weather. If not, use brightly colored crepe paper in thin rolls. It will survive the next storm, but it will most likely disintegrate during the winter.

If you leave any route markers, be sure to **remove your markers** on the return trip. Markers are litter, and good wilderness travelers never, ever litter. If there is any chance that you will not come back the same way and will not be able to remove the markers, be especially sure to use biodegradable markers, if any.

Rock cairns (figure 38) appear here and there as markers, sometimes dotting an entire route and at other times signaling the point where a route changes direction. These heaps of rock are another imposition on the landscape, and they can create confusion for any traveler but the one who put them together—so do not build them. If there ever comes a time when you decide you must, then do so, but be sure to tear them down on the way out. The rule is different, however, for existing cairns. Leave them alone, on the assumption that someone else may be depending on them. Your goal should be to leave the landscape exactly as you found it.

Keep Track

As the trip goes on, it may be helpful to mark your progress on the map. **Keep yourself oriented** so that at any time you can point out your actual position to within about half a mile (roughly 1 kilometer) on the map.

Part of keeping track is having a **sense of your speed**. Given all the variables, will it take your party one hour to travel 2 miles, or will it take two hours to travel 1 mile? The answer is important if it is 3:00 p.m. and base camp is still 5 miles away. After enough trips into the wilds, you will be good at estimating travel speeds. Here are some **typical speeds** for an average party, though there will be much variation:

- Hiking on a gentle trail, with a day pack: 2 to 3 miles (3 to 5 km) per hour
- Climbing up a steep trail, with a full overnight pack: 1 to 2 miles (1.5 to 3 km) per hour
- Traveling up a moderate slope, with a day pack: 1000 feet (about 300 meters) of elevation gain per hour
- Traveling up a moderate slope, with a full overnight pack: 500 feet (about 150 meters) of elevation gain per hour

In heavy brush, your rate of travel can drop to a third or even a quarter of what it would be on a good trail. Above about 10,000 feet (about 3000 m), your rate of travel will also greatly decrease, perhaps to as little as a hundred feet (30 m) of elevation gain per hour, depending on your condition and your state of acclimatization.

On the descent if the terrain is easy, such as on a good trail or a snowfield, your rate of progress can be as much as twice the speed as on the ascent.

With a watch and a notebook (or a really good memory), you can monitor your rate of progress on any outing. Always make sure to note your starting time as well as the times you reach important streams, ridges, trail junctions, and other points along the route.

Experienced wilderness travelers regularly assess their party's progress and compare it with the route plan and the turnaround time. Estimate and re-estimate when you will reach your destination and when you will return to your base camp or starting point. If it begins to look as though your party could become trapped in tricky terrain during darkness, you may discuss the situation with other members of your party and decide to change your plans and bivouac in a safe place or call it a day and return home.

The Return Trip

At your destination: This is your golden opportunity to rest, relax, and enjoy—and to learn more about the area and about map reading by comparing the actual view with the way it looks on the map. Your destination is also the place to **lay final plans for the return**, a journey often responsible for many more routefinding problems than the way in.

- Repeat the trailhead get-together by **discussing the route plan** and emergency strategies with everyone.
- Stress the importance of **keeping the party together** on the return. Invariably, some will want to race ahead while others lag behind.

The return trip is a time for **extra caution** as you fight fatigue and inattention. As on the trip in, everyone needs to maintain a good sense of the route and how it relates to the map. For a safe trip out,

- stay together,
- do not rush, and
- be even more careful if you are taking a different return route.

After the Trip

Back home while the details are fresh in your mind, write a detailed description of the route and any problems, mistakes, or unusual features. Imagine what you would like to know if you were about to do the trip for the first time, so you will be ready with the right answers when another person asks about it. If a guidebook was confusing or wrong, take the time to write to the publisher.

WHAT IF YOU *DO* GET LOST?

Good wilderness travelers are rarely truly lost—but having learned humility through years of experience, they always carry enough food, clothing, and bivouac gear to get them through hours or even days of temporary confusion.

What If Your Party Is Lost?

The first rule is to *stop*. In fact, even if you *think* you may not be where you should be, *stop!*

- Resist the temptation to press onward. The moment you are ever unsure of your position, you should stop.
- Try to determine where you are. Methods of orientation are given in chapter 3.
- Keep your wits about you and do not forget what you have learned about map reading and using the compass, as explained in chapters 1 and 2.
- Study the shape of the terrain and try to associate it with the map to find out where you are.
- Remember the technique of the **bearing of the slope** as explained in Chapter 3. Take a bearing on the fall line and try to associate it with your position by studying the map.

If these suggestions do not work, then try to decide the last time the group *did* know its exact location. If that spot is fairly close, within an hour or so, retrace your steps and get back on route. But if that spot is hours back, you might instead decide to head toward the baseline. If it begins to look as though darkness will fall before you can get back, you might have to bivouac for the night. If so, start looking for an adequate place, with water and some sort of shelter if possible, well before dark.

Being lost in a party is bad enough, but it is even worse when an individual is alone and separated from the rest of the party. For this reason, **always keep the party together**, and assign a rear guard to keep track of any stragglers. If you ever notice that someone is missing, the entire party should stop, stay together, shout, whistle, and listen for answering sounds.

What If You Are Lost Alone?

Again, the first rule is to *stop*. Look around for other members of the party, shout, and listen for answering shouts. Sound your whistle if you have one. If the only answer is silence, sit down, calm down, and combat terror with reason. One of the greatest dangers of being lost is panic, which can lead to making unwise and nonsensical decisions. Once you have calmed down, start doing the right things.

1. **Look at your map** to determine your location and plan a route home.
2. **Mark your location** with branches, a cairn, or other objects (see "Mark the Route If Necessary" above), and then scout in all directions, each time returning to your marked position.
3. **Prepare for the night** by finding water and shelter.
4. **Try singing** so searchers can hear you.

DON'T COUNT ON MOBILE PHONES

Some hikers carry a cell phone into the wilderness for an added level of safety. However, such phones do not work in all locations. They must be able to transmit and receive signals to and from the nearest cell tower, which might be out of range. Coverage in a remote area may also depend on your particular service provider.

The GPS app on your smart phone (see chapter 9) *might* give you your point position, but battery life is limited unless you carry extra batteries or some charging device. Therefore, you should never trust a cell phone to be a dependable way of being rescued if you are injured or lost. Consider cell phones to be unreliable luxuries.

Personal locator beacons (PLBs) and satellite communicators can be very helpful if you become hopelessly lost or need to be rescued due to accident, injury, or illness. See chapter 9 for a description of these GPS-based devices.

The odds are that you will be reunited with your group by morning. If not, fight panic. After a night alone, you may decide to hike out to a baseline feature—a ridge or stream or highway—that you picked out before the trip. If the terrain is too difficult to travel alone, it might be better to concentrate on letting yourself be found. It is far easier for rescuers to find a lost person who stays in one place in the open, sounds a whistle, and shouts periodically, than one who thrashes on in hysterical hope, one step ahead of the rescue party.

The decision **whether to forge ahead or to stay put** is strongly influenced by whether or not **anyone knows that you are missing and where to look for you.** If you are traveling alone, or if your entire party is lost, and no one knows you are missing or where you had planned to go, you have no choice but to try to find your way back, even if this involves difficult travel. If, on the other hand, someone responsible expects you back at a certain time and knows where you were planning to go and what route you planned to take, then you have the option of staying put, making yourself visible, and concentrating on survival while waiting for a search party to find you.

SURVIVAL

Your chances for survival depend on how well equipped you are. Numerous stories of survival and tragedy start with statements such as, "I was sure glad I had my _____," or "Too bad they did not bring a _____." Over the years these crucial items of gear have developed into a codified list known as **The Ten Essentials: A Systems Approach**.

1. **Navigation system**: This contains, at a minimum, a topographic map of the area and a compass. It might also include an altimeter, a GPS receiver, a whistle, and route-marking materials.
2. **Sun protection**: Sunglasses and sunscreen.
3. **Insulation**: Enough extra clothing to survive the most severe night that you can expect in the area you will be visiting.
4. **Illumination system**: A flashlight or headlamp, plus spare batteries and a spare bulb.
5. **First-aid supplies**: Including any prescription medications that you take on a daily basis, in case you do not make it back home in time for the next dose.
6. **Fire system**: Matches in a waterproof case and firestarter.
7. **Repair kit and tools**: At a minimum, a good, multibladed knife. Add other tools depending on what equipment you might need to maintain.

8. **Nutrition**: In addition to snacks, carry enough extra food to survive for at least an additional day more than planned.
9. **Hydration system**: Adequate water plus some water purification method.
10. **Emergency shelter**: A plastic tube tent, for example.

Always consider the possibility that one member of your party might become separated from the rest of the group and will depend totally on his or her own equipment and skill for survival. It is therefore essential that all persons carry adequate food and equipment. It is equally important that all persons in the party have the knowledge and skill to use all the necessary equipment (including the map and compass), rather than always relying on the skills of another. If someone gets lost, having the proper equipment and skills may make the difference between tragedy and a graceful recovery from the experience.

To Sum It Up
It is important to be prepared for unforeseen emergencies such as getting injured or lost, and to have all the equipment and training necessary to survive such an experience. But it is even better to learn the tools of navigation, particularly the map and compass, to avoid getting into such a situation in the first place.

CHAPTER SUMMARY
In this chapter you learned about trip planning and keeping track of your position on the map to ensure that you do not get lost. Additionally, you learned the importance of telling someone responsible where you are going and keeping the party together. Finally, you learned about the gear and a few techniques for getting yourself back on track if you ever do get lost.

SKILLS CHECK

- List three ways to prepare for navigating a trip in the wilderness.
- What essential step should you take before every wilderness trip?
- List three things you should do on the trip itself to avoid getting lost.
- If you think you might be lost, the first thing you should do is _____. (Hint: this is a four-letter word.)
- List three steps you should take if your party is lost.

Chapter
6

More about Maps

CHAPTER OBJECTIVES

- Explain the latitude/longitude coordinate system.
- Describe the UTM coordinate system.
- Discuss other coordinate systems: MGRS and Maidenhead.
- Describe the range, township, and section method of land survey.
- Show how to measure distance on maps.
- Explain how to use pace on wilderness excursions.
- Describe how to measure slope on maps.

USING THE LATITUDE AND LONGITUDE COORDINATE SYSTEM

This familiar system is used, along with UTM, on USGS topographic maps. Only the latitude and longitude (lat/long) system, however, is used on marine charts. Therefore, whereas the land traveler has a choice of using either lat/long or UTM, the nautical traveler using marine charts must know the lat/long system. Lines of constant latitude are sometimes referred to as "parallels" (such as the 49th parallel, which the northern border of Montana follows). Lines of constant longitude are sometimes referred to as "meridians."

Latitude is measured from 0° to 90°, both north and south, from the equator. Longitude is measured from 0° to 180°, both east and west, from the Greenwich meridian, which runs through the Royal Observatory, Greenwich, near London, England. A latitude of north 47°, 12 minutes, and 41.3 seconds would be written N47°12'41.3". This is referred to as the "degrees, minutes, and seconds," or "hddd.mm.ss.s," coordinate system. The "h" defines the hemisphere (i.e., N for north or S for south latitude, and E for east and W for west longitude). Other variations of this system are degrees, minutes, and decimal minutes (hddd.mm.mmm, such as N47°12.6883'), and degrees and decimal degrees (hddd.ddddd, such as N47.2115°). The latter is frequently used by search-and-rescue (SAR) groups.

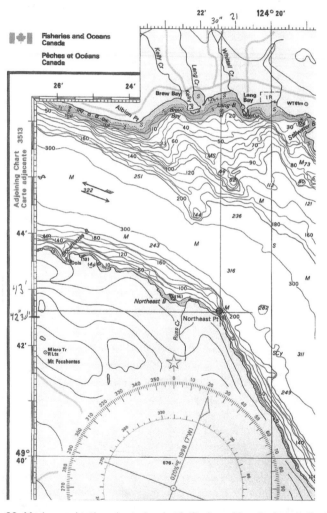

Figure 39. Marine navigation chart showing latitude and longitude coordinates

RELATING LAT/LONG TO MEASUREMENT UNITS

One useful feature of the lat/long system is that **one minute of latitude is equal to one nautical mile**, which is 6076 feet or 1852 meters. Since there are 60 seconds in a minute, this means that **one second of latitude is equivalent to 101 feet, or 34 yards, or 31 meters**. These numbers are often helpful in identifying your position on a topographic map or nautical chart.

The choice of which system to use is often made by looking at the system used on the particular map or marine chart you are using. In figure 39, for example, latitude is shown along the left and right edges of the chart, and longitude is shown along the top and bottom. Note that each minute of latitude and longitude is divided into 10 small divisions. Since one minute equals 60 seconds, the smallest division is therefore 6 seconds (0.10 minute) on this chart. (This relationship is valid for charts with a scale of 1:80,000, a commonly used scale in many areas. However, many different scales are used on marine charts, so the number of seconds or minutes for the smallest division will vary from one chart to another with a different scale.)

The position identified as "Northeast Pt." in figure 39 has north latitude 49°, 42 minutes, and 36 seconds (N49°42'36") and longitude W124°21'24". You can easily find these coordinates by drawing horizontal and vertical lines through the point of interest to the edges of the chart, as shown. The numbers are interpolated from where these lines intersect the scales on the edges of the chart.

SETTING A GPS UNIT TO THE DESIRED COORDINATE SYSTEM

When using a GPS receiver, it is possible to set its coordinate system to either lat/long or UTM. If you are using lat/long, you can then set the display to degrees, minutes, and seconds, or to degrees and decimal degrees, or to degrees, minutes, and decimal minutes in order to match your paper map. This is normally done by using the receiver's "settings" screen. Further details on this subject are given in chapter 9.

It is easier to interpolate between marked divisions if you use degrees, minutes, and decimal minutes. In the above example, since each minute is divided into 10 subdivisions, the smallest division equals 0.10 minute. The point described in this example is seen to have latitude N49°42.6' and longitude W124°21.4'.

USING THE UTM COORDINATE SYSTEM

The Universal Transverse Mercator (UTM) system is a grid of north–south and east–west lines at intervals of 1000 meters (3281 feet or 0.6214 mile), as shown in figure 40, which shows the lower left-hand corner of a typical USGS topographical map. Measurements in the north–south direction are called *northings*, and measurements east and west are called *eastings*. This is far more precise for USGS topo maps

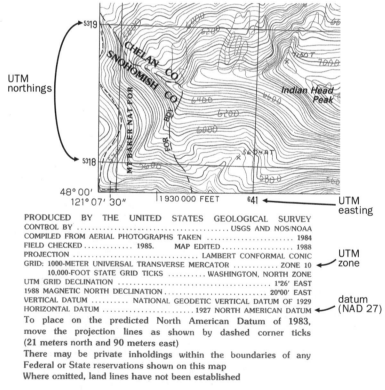

Figure 40. Lower left corner of a USGS topographic map showing UTM zone and horizontal datum; UTM partial eastings and northings also shown

than the lat/long system, because USGS maps only identify latitude and longitude coordinates every 2.5 minutes (approximately 2 to 3 miles or 3 to 5 kilometers). Without using a scale or ruler, you can usually "eyeball" your position to within about 100 meters (about 300 feet) using UTM, which is often close enough to at least get to within sight of your objective. If greater precision is desired, you can use the meters scale at the bottom of the map, or special map measurement tools.

METRIC CONVERSIONS

For most practical purposes, you can think of a meter as being approximately equal to a yard. Actually, 1 yard (36 inches) is equal to 0.9144 meter, and 1 meter equals 1.094 yards. If you need to do exact conversions, 1 inch equals 2.54 centimeters, and there are 100 centimeters in a meter and 1000 meters in 1 kilometer (km). One km is the same as 0.6214 miles, and 1 mile equals 1.609 km. One meter equals 3.2808 feet, and 1 foot equals 0.3048 meters. (It's pretty easy these days to find digital conversion charts online that are at least roughly accurate.)

A **northing** is the number of meters north or south of the equator. An **easting** is the number of meters east of a certain reference line. This line is based on the **zone** number and the **datum**. These important numbers are shown in the lower left corner of the map, as in figure 40. These will be described in more detail later in this chapter, but at this point we wish to give a practical example so that you can appreciate how the system works.

For example, suppose you are climbing toward Glacier Peak in Washington state, and clouds obscure all visibility. You reach a summit but are not sure whether it is the true summit of Glacier Peak. You turn on your GPS receiver and let it acquire a position. The UTM numbers on the screen of your GPS receiver are as follows:

10 6 40 612E

53 29 491N

The top number is the easting. The "10" is the UTM zone number. The numbers "6 40 612E" indicate your position within zone 10. In figure 41, you can find the number "6 40 000mE" along the top edge of the map. This is the *full easting* (except for the zone number). To

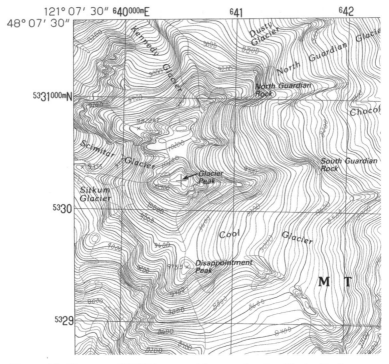

Figure 41. Close-up of USGS topographic map showing Glacier Peak summit area

the right of this is the number 6 41. This is a *partial easting*, with the "000" meters omitted. You can see that the number "10 6 40 612E" on the screen of the GPS receiver is approximately six-tenths of the way between 6 40 000 and 6 41 000. Your east–west position is therefore about six-tenths of the way between the 6 40 000 and the 6 41 lines. Your position is somewhere on a line running roughly through both Glacier Peak and Disappointment Peak.

Along the left edge of the map shown in figure 41 is the number "53 31 000mN." This is the *full northing*, which indicates that this point is 5,331,000 meters north of the equator. Below this is a line labeled "53 30," and another labeled "53 29." These are *partial northings*, with the "000" meters omitted. The second set of numbers displayed on the GPS receiver is 53 29 491N. This is a horizontal line about halfway between 53 29 and 53 30. The point where the easting and the northing lines intersect is your *point position*. Finding this point in figure 41 shows that you are on Disappointment Peak. (Sorry; keep climbing.)

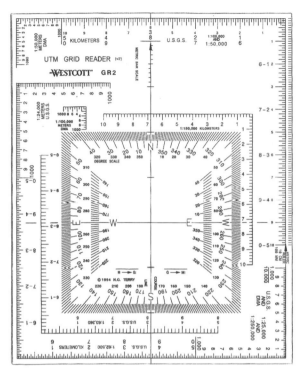

Figure 42. An example of a plastic scale to measure UTM position

If you have difficulty "eye-balling" distances between UTM coordinate lines, there are special rulers and other measuring devices that you can use instead. You can purchase special plastic scales to read UTM coordinates on 1:24,000-scale (7.5-minute) maps (see figure 42), though this requires carrying one more piece of special equipment. Some compasses are equipped with special scales to locate your position on maps; some of these have "GPS" in their model numbers. Other

Figure 43. An example of a compass with roamer scales

compasses have "roamer" (sometimes spelled "romer") scales for use with either 1:24,000- or 1:50,000-scale maps. The compass shown in figure 43, for example, has roamer scales for 1:25,000- and 1:50,000-scale maps, as used on metric maps. A similar compass made for use in the United States would have roamers for 1:24,000- and 1:63,360-scale maps.

You can make a homemade scale by photocopying the meters scale at the bottom of a USGS topo map, cutting out the desired scale, and gluing it to a piece of heavy paper (see figure 44).

Any of these techniques will allow you to get better accuracy than merely "eyeballing" the map.

Figure 44. Homemade map distance scale

NAVIGATION USING GPS AND UTM COORDINATES

Suppose that you can identify your desired destination on the map but cannot actually see it in the field. You can then read the UTM position of the destination off the map and enter it into your GPS memory as a waypoint. You can then get the GPS receiver to tell you the distance and direction to that place.

Going back to the Glacier Peak example shown in figure 41, suppose you wish to find the route from wherever you are to the summit of Glacier Peak. From the map, you can see that the summit of Glacier Peak is about halfway between the eastings of 6 40 000 and 6 41 000, so you could estimate the easting as 10 6 40 500 (the zone number is still 10). You can also see that the summit is about three-tenths of the way between the northings of 53 30 000 and 53 31 000, so you can estimate the full northing to be 53 30 300N. You can now enter the UTM coordinates of 10 6 40 500E and 53 30 300N into your GPS receiver.

Navigation using GPS, map, and compass is discussed more thoroughly in chapter 9.

DATUM, ZONE, AND LATITUDE BANDS

A *datum* is a point of reference used by mapmakers, surveyors, and GPS device manufacturers, upon which to base position coordinates. The most recent horizontal datum, the one used by the Global Positioning System, is denoted as WGS84 (World Geodetic System, 1984). This is most GPS receivers' default datum and is appropriate for most USGS topographic maps being produced today.

Older datums are used on many other maps such as NAD27 CONUS (North American Datum 1927 for the Continental United States), NAD27 Alaska, NAD27 Canada, NAD83, and others. The datum is usually printed in the lower left-hand corner of the map (see figure 40, in which NAD27 is identified as the map's horizontal datum).

Before you use a GPS receiver with any topo map, you must first find the map's datum, and go to the receiver's setup or settings screen to get a list of all its available map datums. Then **select the datum that agrees with the map's datum.** Failure to use the proper datum can result in errors of as much as several hundred meters or yards.

The **UTM** *zone* is usually printed on USGS maps (see figure 40, for zone 10). There are 60 zones, and each is 6° wide. Zone 1 is for the area from 180° W longitude to 174° W, and its zone meridian (centerline) is 177° W. Zone 2 is from 174° W to 168° W longitude, with a zone meridian of 171° W, and so on. The centerline of each zone is numbered 5 00 000mE. The reference for UTM eastings is a meridian located 500,000 meters west of the zone meridian.

Some GPS receivers use a *latitude band* letter with UTM to indicate position relative to the equator. This system divides Earth into 8°-wide latitude bands from 80° S latitude to 84° N latitude (the northernmost band being a bit wider than the others). The bands are lettered from south to north, according to the following table:

Table 5. Latitude Bands and Latitude Ranges

Band	Range	Band	Range
C	72–80 South	N	0–8 North
D	64–72 South	P	8–16 North
E	56–64 South	Q	16–24 North
F	48–56 South	R	24–32 North
G	40–48 South	S	32–40 North
H	32–40 South	T	40–48 North
J	24–32 South	U	48–56 North
K	16–24 South	V	56–64 North
L	8–16 South	W	64–72 North
M	0–8 South	X	72–84 North

If the latitude band is used, the letter for that band is placed immediately after the zone number, such as 10T 05 46 379. Some GPS receivers require using such a latitude band. Others merely ask you to indicate which hemisphere you are in, north or south.

Due to distortion of the UTM grid lines near the poles, UTM is not defined north of N84° or south of S80° latitude.

CONVERTING BETWEEN LAT/LONG AND UTM

If you ever need to convert from one of these systems to another, you can enter coordinates in one system into a GPS receiver, then change its settings to the other desired system, and the receiver will make the conversion for you. Without a GPS receiver, you can find coordinate conversion websites on the internet by entering "lat/long to UTM convert" into the search engine of your choice. Two such sites are www.earthpoint.us /Convert.aspx and www.ngs.noaa.gov/TOOLS/utm.shtml.

OTHER COORDINATE SYSTEMS

The area covered by UTM includes most of the world except Antarctica and arctic regions north of Alaska's north coast. In those areas you can use the lat/long grid or the UPS grid instead.

The Universal Polar Stereographic (UPS) grid is very similar to the UTM grid, in that it expresses locations with a grid of 1-kilometer squares, and eastings and northings expressed in meters, just as with UTM. Some GPS receivers have a single setting for both, such as "UTM/ UPS" or "UTM UPS." The zone number is always zero for the UPS grid. The latitude band letters are A or B for the Antarctic region, and Y and Z for the arctic region. Most GPS devices automatically switch from UTM to UPS when traveling north of N84° or south of S80°.

Since nautical charts and USGS topographic maps only use latitude/ longitude and UTM or UPS, those systems are all that you need to know for wilderness travel. But in case you wonder what some of the other systems referred to on GPS receivers are, we will briefly mention three additional systems.

The Military Grid Reference System (MGRS) is used by the US military. It is essentially the same as the UTM system, except that some

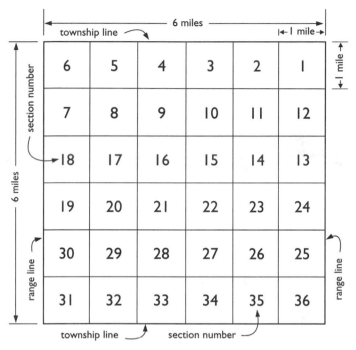

Figure 45. A township consists of a square 6 miles on a side that contains 36 sections. Each side of each section is one mile.

of the leading UTM numbers are replaced by letters. **The last five digits of the MGRS easting and northing are the same as for UTM.** For example, if your UTM location is 10T 04 71523E and 53 07108N, your MRGS location is expressed as 10T DJ 71523 and 07108. Note that the "71523" and the "07108" are the same in each system. The only difference is that the first two digits of the UTM easting and northing are replaced by letters.

MGRS Polar is similar to the UPS grid, based on a grid of 1-kilometer squares for the polar areas outside the area of coverage for MGRS.

Maidenhead is a grid used by amateur radio operators, based on 1-kilometer squares just as the UTM system. For the location in the paragraph above, the Maidenhead coordinates are given by CN87HW.

RANGE, TOWNSHIP, AND SECTION

The primary surveying system used in most parts of the United States is the Range, Township, and Section system. In this system, most of the

Figure 46. Marker on the Willamette Stone near Portland, Oregon, the center of the range, township, and section system of land surveying in Oregon and Washington

United States is divided into regions called townships. This system is used in all the states west of the Mississippi River (except for Texas), as well as in Minnesota, Wisconsin, Michigan, Ohio, Indiana, Illinois, Mississippi, Alabama, and Florida.

A **township** is a 36-square-mile area. The township is divided into 36 one-square-mile **sections**. The sections are numbered from 1 to 36 in a zigzag pattern starting at the northeast corner of the township (see figure 45).

Each section is divided into **quarter-sections**, such as the "northeast quarter of section 23." If necessary, these quarter-sections are sometimes further subdivided, such as "the southeast quarter of the northwest quarter of section 23" of a particular township. In this way, a certain location can be pinpointed to within a quarter of a mile. This method is often used to define property boundaries.

Each township is identified by its location with respect to a baseline and a meridian in a local coordinate system.

One example is the Willamette Baseline and the Principal Willamette Meridian, whose intersection is located in Willamette Stone State Park near Portland, Oregon (see figure 46). This point is used as the basis of the range, township, and section system throughout the states of Washington and Oregon. The location of each township in these states is referred to by its distance from the intersection of the Principal Willamette Meridian (a north–south line) and the Willamette Baseline (an east–west line; see figure 47). A township whose northern boundary is three townships (18 miles) north of the Willamette Baseline is identified as T3N. If this area's eastern boundary is 30 miles east of the Principal Willamette Meridian, the township is identified as R5E. If a specific location within this township is in Section 23, it is identified as Section 23, Township 3N, Range 5E, or Section 23, T3N, R5E.

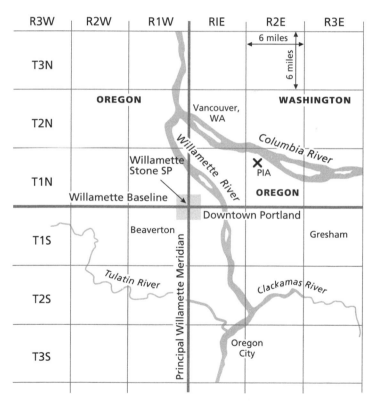

Figure 47. *In the states of Washington and Oregon, township line boundaries are defined based on their distance north or south of the Willamette Baseline. Range line boundaries are defined based on their distance east or west of the Principal Willamette Meridian. These lines intersect just west of Portland in Willamette Stone State Park.*

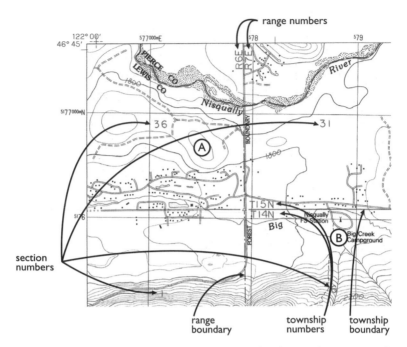

Figure 48. A portion of a USGS topographic map, showing section, range, and township numbers and boundaries

In locations where the land has been surveyed using this method, the boundaries between sections, townships, and ranges are usually indicated by light red lines on USGS topographic maps. The township and range boundaries are shown by red letters and numbers such as R5E or T6N near the edges of the maps. The sections are numbered from 1 to 36 with red numbers in the centers of the sections. In figure 48, for example, the hill indicated by A is in Section 36, T15N, R6E. Big Creek Campground (indicated by B) is in Section 6, T14N, R7E.

Some areas in the United States have not yet been surveyed. In these areas, the range, township, section system cannot be used. In this case, locations can be specified using the lat/long system or the UTM system.

Property surveys, timber sales, and some other forestry-related applications often use the section, township, and range system, though this system is not available on all GPS receivers.

DISTANCE MEASUREMENT ON A MAP

You can easily measure distances on a map using the scales at the bottom of it. To measure a **straight-line distance**, simply measure the length of the line joining the two points of interest using a **scale of your compass**. Then transfer this distance to one of the scales at the bottom of the map and read off the number of feet, meters, kilometers, or miles. If the distance on the map is greater than the length of your compass scale, or if the route is **not a straight line**, then you can instead use the **lanyard** attached to your compass. (If your compass does not have a lanyard, you can easily create one by tying a shoelace or other cord to the compass through the hole made for the lanyard.) Put the free end of the lanyard on one point on the map, then place the lanyard on the route to be measured, curving it along the trail, ridge, or other feature, until it reaches the other point on the map. Then straighten out the lanyard and place it alongside the desired scale at the bottom of the map.

While following trails with numerous short switchbacks, this method may be inaccurate, since the lanyard may not be able to keep up with all the tiny zigzags. In this case, your map measurement will at least give you a minimum distance, which may be enough information for your purposes.

Suppose you want to find the distance from Blue Lake to Johnson Mountain as shown in figure 49. You can measure the straight-line distance from the lake's outlet at its southwest tip to the summit of Johnson Mountain to find out how far a trip it would be. If you place

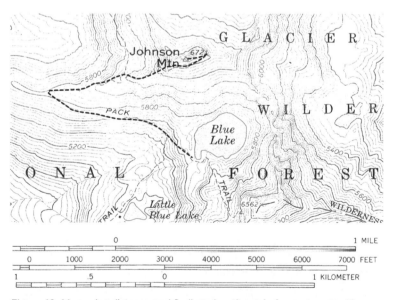

Figure 49. Measuring distance and finding elevation gain from a topographic map

the scale of your compass along this route, you can get a certain map distance, in inches, centimeters, or millimeters, whatever you prefer. Placing the compass along the scales at the bottom of the map shows that this corresponds to about 0.4 mile or 2200 feet (0.7 kilometer or 700 meters). (Try it yourself, and see if you agree!)

Note that there is a trail from Blue Lake to the summit of Johnson Mountain. Though the distance to the peak will be longer via the trail, the travel will most certainly be easier. You can measure the distance along the trail by placing the free end of the lanyard on the map at the outlet of Blue Lake, then curving the lanyard along the trail until it reaches the summit of Johnson Mountain. Then straighten out the lanyard and place it alongside whatever scale you want to use at the bottom of the map. The distance corresponds to about 1.3 miles or 7000 feet (2.1 km or 2100 m). Try it. Do you agree?

You can use either feet and miles, or meters and kilometers for measuring or pacing distances. However, metric units are much easier to use, since you can mentally convert distances from kilometers to meters and vice versa, by multiplying or dividing by 1000. Converting miles to feet or vice versa, on the other hand, requires multiplying or dividing by 5280 (the number of feet in a mile), which can be time-consuming and cumbersome in the field.

PACE

It is occasionally necessary to go a certain distance in a given direction, for example, 300 feet (100 m) in a northeasterly direction. Doing this requires a good estimate of your pace. All wilderness travelers should have a rough idea of the length of their pace. The length of your normal pace is the distance you cover when you walk two steps (one step with each foot) on level ground at a comfortable walking stride. To measure your normal pace, establish a starting point where you will be able to walk in a straight line on level terrain. Walk for 10 full paces (10 steps with each foot), and mark the place where you stopped. Then measure the distance you walked. Divide that distance by 10 to get the length of your pace. For example, if the distance for 10 full paces is 50 feet, then your pace is 5 feet. The normal pace for most people ranges from 3 to 6 feet (about 1 to 2 meters).

Once you know your pace, you can use it to travel a given distance in the field. Suppose you want to travel 1000 feet, and you know your pace is 5 feet. Divide 1000 feet by 5 feet per pace, and the result is 200 paces. This sort of calculation is best done at home before the trip, as a part of preparing a route plan, if done at all.

> **TIP:** When using the length of pace in your travels, keep in mind that your actual pace will vary considerably due to differences in terrain. For example, your pace will be shorter when going uphill or through heavy brush, and longer when descending a good trail. So whenever you use your pace in navigation, be sure to make allowances for variations in the length of your pace with the terrain.

Counting paces is a poor way to travel in the wilderness, since it is easy to lose count. If you concentrate hard enough to avoid losing count, you may miss important details of the route, such as key topographic features, and it may detract from your enjoyment of the trip. Keeping track of your location is far better achieved by watching the topography. If counting paces is necessary at all, we recommend that you use it only for short distances.

SLOPE (GRADE) MEASUREMENT ON A MAP

By carefully measuring the distance between contour lines on a topographic map, you can estimate the steepness, or **grade**, of the slope as a percentage. We can find the grade of the slope by finding the **vertical distance**, or elevation gain, **divided by the horizontal distance, and multiplying the result by 100.** This knowledge is important in estimating the risk of avalanches (see "On Snow" in chapter 10) and for determining the feasibility of a particular route. You can do this in the field, but it is easiest if done at home before your trip.

In the example shown in figure 49, we found the straight-line distance from Blue Lake to Johnson Mountain to be about 2200 feet. The elevation of Johnson Mountain is 6721 feet (as shown on the map), and the elevation of Blue Lake is 5625 feet. Subtracting 5625 from 6721 gives an elevation gain of 1096 feet. If you were to travel in a straight line from Blue Lake to Johnson Mountain, the **grade** of the slope would be the elevation gain (1096 feet) divided by the horizontal distance (2200 feet), multiplied by 100. This gives a grade of about 50 percent, which is a very steep grade; traveling along this route will be difficult and possibly dangerous. Note also that this 50 percent is merely an **average grade**. The first 200 feet of gain will be rather gentle, but the next 400 feet will be steeper, as can be inferred from the closer contour lines. Above 6200 feet, the slope eases up somewhat. Since the average grade is 50 percent and some of the route has a lesser grade, it is apparent that the steepest grade along this route will be even more than 50 percent.

If you instead take the trail from Blue Lake to Johnson Mountain, the elevation gain is the same: 1096 feet. But the distance that you measured earlier using the lanyard of the compass was about 7000 feet. The average grade along the trail is therefore 1096 divided by 7000, multiplied by 100, or about 16 percent. This is a much more reasonable grade than that of the straight-line route, and it will probably be an enjoyable hike rather than a difficult and possibly dangerous climb.

These examples illustrate how to find the average grade over some distance. You can also find the *steepest* grade along any route using a similar procedure. Draw a line on the map indicating your proposed route. Pick out the place on this line that appears to be the steepest: the place where the contour lines are closest together. Identify two particular contour lines in this area—for example, two index contours

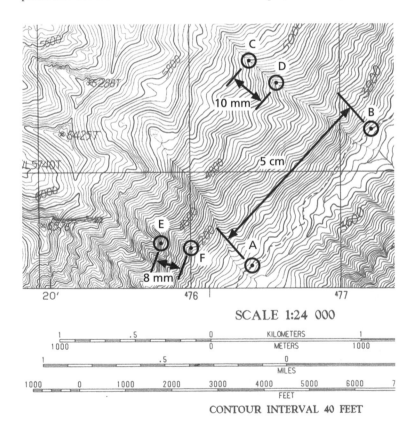

SCALE 1:24 000

CONTOUR INTERVAL 40 FEET

Figure 50. Measuring grade on a map

(indicated by the heavier contour lines). The difference between these two lines is the vertical height of the slope. Now measure the horizontal distance between these same two lines with the scale of your compass (or any other suitable device). Transfer this measurement to the feet scale at the bottom of the map. Then you can find the steepest grade of the slope by making the same calculation as above.

If you have a metric map, the contour interval will be in meters instead of feet. In this case, your horizontal distance must also be in meters. Use whatever units you want, as long as you use the same units for both the vertical and the horizontal measurements.

Figure 50 shows several examples of measuring the grade of the slope. Points A and B are at elevations of 3600 and 3400 feet, so the vertical height is 3600 minus 3400, or 200 feet. The horizontal distance on the map, which can be measured with a ruler, is found to be 5 centimeters. Transferring this to the scale for feet at the bottom of the map gives a distance of 3800 feet. The grade is 200 feet divided by 3800 feet, multiplied by 100, or 0.05 multiplied by 100, which equals 5 percent. This is a gentle slope.

Points C and D are at elevations of 5000 feet and 4600 feet, so the vertical height is 400 feet. The horizontal distance is 10 millimeters, which, when transferred to the scale for feet, gives 800 feet. The grade is 400 feet divided by 800 feet, multiplied by 100, which equals 50 percent, a steep slope. A grade of 50 percent corresponds to approximately a 27° angle.

Points E and F are at elevations of 4800 feet and 4200 feet. The vertical height is 600 feet. The horizontal distance on the map is 8 millimeters, corresponding to a distance of 600 feet, which is the same as the vertical height of 600 feet. The grade is 100 percent—a 45° angle. This is a very steep slope. If the vertical height is equal to the horizontal distance, the grade is 100 percent, and the angle of the slope is 45°.

Instead of measuring horizontal distances with a ruler, you can just as easily calculate the distance by making two pencil marks on a scrap of paper, corresponding to the horizontal distance on the map between the two contour lines. Then move this paper alongside the appropriate scale at the bottom of the map to convert that distance to feet or meters.

Measuring the grade of the slope is easy; it merely requires dividing the vertical height by the horizontal distance (sometimes called "rise over run"). But expressing the result as an **angle**, in degrees, requires the use of trigonometry, which we would rather avoid in the field. For your information, the relationship between slope grade and slope angle is shown in table 6 below:

Table 6. Slope Grade and Slope Angle

% Grade	Angle (in degrees)	% Grade	Angle (in degrees)
0%	0°	90%	42°
10%	6°	100%	45°
20%	11°	120%	50°
30%	17°	140%	54°
40%	22°	170%	60°
50%	27°	200%	63°
60%	31°	250%	68°
70%	35°	300%	72°
80%	39°	400%	76°

You can use this table (or trigonometry if you know it) for trip planning at home, but in the field you usually only need to know a few values. A 20 percent grade is representative of a reasonably steep trail, such as one that gains about 1000 feet in 1 mile. A 50 percent grade has an angle of 27°, and a 100 percent grade has an angle of 45°. These three numbers can help you to determine the feasibility of negotiating a particular slope and can also help you to assess the risk of avalanche hazard (see "On Snow" in chapter 10). A 50 percent grade is a very steep slope, well past the limit for hiking. Slopes steeper than 50 percent usually involve difficult scrambling or climbing. By the time the grade gets to 100 percent, the terrain is usually too steep for unroped travel, and you will probably need to belay for safety. On snow, you may need an ice ax even if the grade is less than 30 percent.

All wilderness travelers should **know their limits when it comes to slope**. Sometime when you are going up or down a slope that appears to be at your limit, and you feel uncomfortable about being on any steeper terrain, mark that spot on your map. Once you get home, measure the grade of that slope for that location on the map as mentioned above. Then you will know your limit, and the next time you contemplate a route in unfamiliar territory, you will be able to measure its grade on the map to find out if it is within your limits.

CHAPTER SUMMARY

In this chapter, you have learned the details of the lat/long and UTM systems of defining positions on a map, as well as some basic aspects of other coordinate systems. The range, township, and section system of land surveying was also described. We also explained how to measure distance and slope, or grade, from maps, and how to measure and use your pace in your travels.

SKILLS CHECK

- What are the approximate latitude and longitude coordinates of your home?
- One second of latitude corresponds to how many feet, yards, or meters?
- What do the letters UTM stand for?
- In the UTM grid on a 7.5-minute USGS map, what is the distance, in meters, between grid lines?
- How do you measure the grade, or slope, of an area on a topo map?

PRACTICE PROBLEMS *See the appendix for problem instructions.*

- Problems 2, 3, 5, 6, 10, 11, 13, 14, 29, and 30 will give you practice in the principles covered in this chapter.

Chapter
7

More about Compasses and Geomagnetism

CHAPTER OBJECTIVES

- Explain how to get accurate declination information.
- Describe how and why declination is changing.
- Explain compass dip and how to cope with it.
- Show how to use clinometers.
- Describe some types of compasses not covered in chapter 2.

Chapter 2 provided a general introduction to the subject of compasses, explained how to use a compass to take and follow bearings in the field, and how to measure and plot bearings on a map. The present chapter goes deeper into the subject of geomagnetism and compass use, by providing detailed information on compasses and geomagnetism.

WHERE TO GET DECLINATION INFORMATION

To find the declination for any point in the United States, call the USGS at 303-273-8487. For Canada, call the Geological Survey of Canada at 613-837-4241.

Declination information is also available on the internet. The National Oceanic and Atmospheric Administration (NOAA) website, www.ngdc.noaa.gov/geomag/calculators/magcalc.shtml, provides declination information for any place in the United States with only the postal ZIP code or the latitude/longitude coordinates of the location. The latter can be found by looking at any corner of a USGS topographic map for the area of interest. There are also drop-down menus for major cities in the United States and other countries. In addition to giving the magnetic declination in degrees, this website provides the present amount of annual change in declination and provides declination maps of the world.

DECLINATION OUTSIDE NORTH AMERICA

On the NOAA website, the default latitude and longitude are north latitude and west longitude, which is appropriate for North America. It is possible, however, to enter southern latitudes and eastern longitudes, and therefore to find the declination for any point on the surface of the Earth. The website can also give you declination for any year from 1900 to 2025; this time span is increased as time progresses.

Another useful website is the Canadian Geomagnetic Reference Field (CGRF), https://geomag.nrcan.gc.ca/calc/mdcal-en.php. This site gives you present declination and its rate of change when you enter a set of latitude and longitude coordinates. It also has drop-down menus for all major cities in Canada. The CGRF can also give you declination for any year from 1900 to 2025; this time span is increased as time progresses.

TIP: The CGRF is specifically optimized for use in Canada, but it works just as well for the United States and elsewhere. The CGRF data input assumes that all latitudes are north and all longitudes are west. But it also allows southern latitudes and eastern longitudes, so it can provide declination information for any place in the world.

Both of the above-mentioned websites provide additional interesting and useful information on declination and compass use.

In most parts of the world, you can buy topographic maps with declination information. If you go to a foreign country where you cannot find the declination, and if you do not have internet access, you can

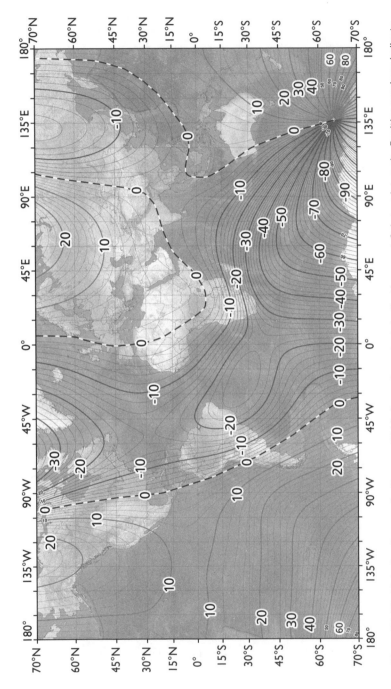

Figure 51. World declination map for the year 2015: lines of constant declination are at 2-degree intervals. Positive numbers indicate east declination; negative numbers indicate west declination.

find a fairly close estimate of the declination from the world declination map shown in figure 51 (source: NOAA magnetic declination website, http://maps.ngdc.noaa.gov/viewers/historical_declination/).

CHANGES IN DECLINATION

Magnetic declination is caused by the motion of magnetic material in Earth's core. The soil and rock upon which we live is only a relatively thin crust. Beneath it a solid **mantle** of rock extending to about 1800 miles (2900 kilometers). Beneath this is a molten interior more than a thousand miles thick. In the center of our planet there is a solid inner core, rotating at a slightly different rate than the outer mantle. This rotation causes the molten material between the two solid portions to move. Since this material is magnetic (predominantly iron), its constant motion creates a **slowly varying magnetic field**.

The motion of the molten magnetic material is mostly random and unpredictable, so we cannot predict with certainty what the declination will be at any given place far in the future. However, Earth is very large, and changes take place slowly. Declination and its rate of change can therefore be studied and recorded over long periods of time to arrive at mathematical models that predict declination over a relatively short period of time, such as just a few years in the future. This is the basis for the declination prediction models referred to above.

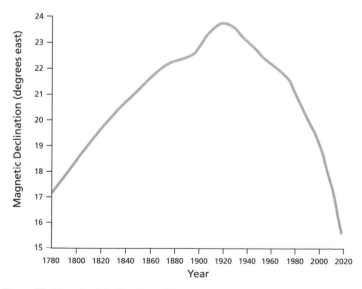

Figure 52. Historical declination of Seattle

One example of how declination has changed over time is shown in figure 52, a graph showing the declination in Seattle, Washington, over the past two centuries, based on information from the NOAA website listed above. You can obtain similar information for any other chosen location from the NOAA site. From the main web page, find and click on the "US Historic Declination" tab. Then enter the range of dates and the location, and you should get a tabular listing of magnetic declination for your location for as long a time period as declination has been measured in the past.

It is very helpful for you to know how rapidly magnetic declination is changing for your area of interest. This knowledge will enable you to evaluate the accuracy of declination data printed on older maps, and to know how frequently you need to make adjustments or modifications to your compass. You can obtain this information from either of the above websites, since both provide the declination rate of change as well as the declination once you provide the coordinates and desired date. If the rate of change is given in minutes per year, and you want to get the rate of change in degrees per year, divide the number of minutes by 60. For example, a rate of change of 7.2 minutes per year is 7.2 divided by 60, or 0.12 degree per year. The reciprocal of this value (1 divided by 0.12) is the number of years for a 1° change; in this example, 8.3 years. This means that in this example, the declination is forecast to change by 1° in the next 8.3 years.

If the rate of change is in the **same direction as your declination** (for example, if declination is east and rate of change is east), then the numerical value of declination is increasing. If the rate of change and the declination are in **opposite directions** (for example, east declination and westerly rate of change), then the numerical value of declination will be **decreasing**.

Table 7 below is a listing of magnetic declination, its rate of change, and the time period required for a 1° declination change, for one location in every state and province in the United States and Canada. A glance at this table will give you at least a rough idea of how much the declination is changing in your area. You can see, for example, that declination is barely changing at all in many of the mid-Atlantic states, Hawaii, and southern Ontario, whereas it is changing much more rapidly in Alaska, the northern states from Washington to North Dakota, and in the western provinces from British Columbia to Saskatchewan.

Some wilderness travelers pencil in the current declination, along with its year and month, on their paper topo maps for future reference.

Table 7. Declination and Its Rate of Change, United States and Canada, 2025

US State or Canadian Province	City	Declination	Annual Declination Change and Direction	Number of Years to Change 1°
Alabama	Montgomery	4° W	0.08° W	12
Alaska	Fairbanks	15° E	0.3° W	3
Alberta	Calgary	14° E	0.10° W	10
Arizona	Phoenix	10° E	0.10° W	10
Arkansas	Little Rock	0°	0.1° W	10
British Columbia	Prince George	17° E	0.12° W	9
California	Sacramento	13° E	0.08° W	12
Colorado	Denver	8° E	0.1° W	12
Connecticut	Hartford	13° W	0.05° E	20
Delaware	Dover	12° W	0.02° W	> 20
Florida	Jacksonville	7° W	0.07° W	15
Georgia	Atlanta	6° W	0.07° W	15
Hawaii	Honolulu	9° E	0.0°	> 20
Idaho	Boise	13° E	0.10° W	10
Illinois	Springfield	2° W	0.07° W	15
Indiana	Indianapolis	5° W	0.05° W	20
Iowa	Des Moines	0°	0.07° W	15
Kansas	Topeka	2° E	0.08° W	12
Kentucky	Frankfort	6° W	0.05° W	20
Louisiana	Baton Rouge	1° W	0.10° W	10
Maine	Augusta	15° W	0.10° E	10
Manitoba	Winnipeg	3° E	0.05° W	20
Maryland	Annapolis	11° W	0.0°	> 20
Massachusetts	Boston	14° W	0.067° E	15
Michigan	Lansing	7° W	0.0°	> 20

US State or Canadian Province	City	Declination	Annual Declination Change and Direction	Number of Years to Change 1°
Minnesota	Minneapolis	0°	0.05° W	20
Mississippi	Jackson	2° W	0.10° W	10
Missouri	Jefferson City	1° W	0.08° W	12
Montana	Billings	10° E	0.08° W	12
Nebraska	Lincoln	3° E	0.08° W	12
Nevada	Las Vegas	11° E	0.1° W	10
New Brunswick	Fredericton	16° W	0.13° E	8
Newfoundland	St. John's	17° W	0.18° E	5
New Hampshire	Concord	14° W	0.08° E	12
New Jersey	Trenton	12° W	0.03° E	> 20
New Mexico	Santa Fe	8° E	0.10° W	10
New York	Syracuse	12° W	0.05° E	20
North Carolina	Raleigh	9° W	0.03° W	> 20
North Dakota	Bismarck	6° E	0.08° W	12
Nova Scotia	Halifax	16° W	0.13° E	8
Ohio	Columbus	7° W	0.03° W	> 20
Oklahoma	Oklahoma City	3° E	0.10° W	10
Ontario	Toronto	10° W	0.02° E	> 20
Oregon	Bend	14° E	0.08° W	12
Pennsylvania	Harrisburg	11° W	0.02° E	> 20
Prince Edward Island	Charlottetown	17° W	0.15° E	7
Quebec	Montreal	14° W	0.08° E	12
Rhode Island	Providence	14° W	0.07° E	15
Saskatchewan	Regina	8° E	0.07° W	15
South Carolina	Columbia	8° W	0.05° W	20
South Dakota	Pierre	5° E	0.08° W	12

US State or Canadian Province	City	Declination	Annual Declination Change and Direction	Number of Years to Change 1°
Tennessee	Nashville	4° W	0.07° W	15
Texas	Austin	3° E	0.12° W	9
Utah	Salt Lake City	11° E	0.10° W	10
Vermont	Montpelier	14° W	0.08° E	12
Virginia	Richmond	10° W	0.0° W	› 20
Washington	Olympia	15° E	0.10° W	10
West Virginia	Charleston	8° W	0.03° W	› 20
Wisconsin	Madison	3° W	0.05° W	20
Wyoming	Casper	9° E	0.10° W	10

Note: If declination and declination change are both in the same direction (as for Alabama, where both are W), then the amount of declination is presently increasing. Therefore, in twelve years, the declination in Alabama is projected to be about 5° W. If declination and declination change are in opposite directions (as for Wyoming, where declination is E but declination change is W), then the amount of declination is presently decreasing. So in ten years, the declination in Wyoming is projected to be about 8° E.

DIP

The magnetic needle of the compass is not only affected by the horizontal direction of Earth's magnetic field but also by its vertical pull. The closer you get to the magnetic north pole, the more the north-seeking end of the needle tends to point downward. At the magnetic equator, the needle will be level, while at the south magnetic pole the north-seeking end of the needle tries to point in an upward direction. This phenomenon is referred to as **compass dip**. To compensate for this effect, most compass manufacturers purposely introduce a slight imbalance to the magnetic needles of their compasses, so that their dip is negligible **for the geographic area where they will be used**. Earth is divided into several **dip zones**, and compasses sold in each zone may be compensated for use in that zone.

If you buy a compass in one dip zone and try to use it in another, the compass may not work well because of the difference in dip. For example, if you buy a compass in North America or Europe and then try to use it in the southern hemisphere, the difference in dip may be enough to introduce errors in your compass readings or even make the compass impossible to use.

TEST YOUR COMPASS FOR THE EFFECTS OF DIP

If you bring your compass to a faraway place, you should first try it out in an urban area as soon as you arrive there, to make sure it works properly before heading out into the wilderness. If it is adversely affected by dip, you may have to buy a new compass in the general area where you will be traveling before leaving town.

To avoid problems with dip, you can buy a compass ahead of time that is properly compensated for dip in the area you will be visiting. Some retail stores and mail-order companies have, or can order, compasses compensated for whatever zone you will be visiting.

Some manufacturers produce compasses that are not affected by dip. These compasses have the term "**global**" in their names, or a notation on the package that the compass is corrected for dip anywhere in the world. If you intend to go on worldwide adventures, you might consider purchasing such a compass. Tables 1 and 2 in chapter 2 identify some such compasses.

USING A CLINOMETER

Some compasses are equipped with a **clinometer**, which measures angles of slope, or elevation angles, using a gravity-assisted needle. To use the clinometer on your compass, follow these steps:

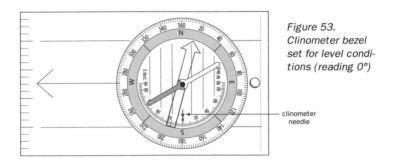

Figure 53. Clinometer bezel set for level conditions (reading 0°)

clinometer needle

1. First, hold the compass with its long edge horizontal, and turn the bezel so that the numbered inside scale (usually the same scale used for declination adjustment) is at the lower long edge of the compass (see figure 53).
2. Set either 90° or 270° at the index line, so that the needle points to zero when it is held level. (If the direction-of-travel arrow is pointing from right to left, as in figure 53, then you will set 270° at the index line. If it is pointing from left to right, you will set 90° at the index line.)
3. Then, tilting the compass up or down will cause the clinometer needle to point to the number of degrees upward or downward.

There are **two ways to use the clinometer**. The first is to measure the **elevation angle** to a distant object. For example, suppose you are at the summit of a peak, and you see another peak of nearly the same elevation. You wonder if you are on the higher of the two summits. Hold the compass with its long edge pointing toward the other peak, as you sight along the long edge of the baseplate (see figure 54). Steady the compass on a rock or other stable object if possible. Tap the compass lightly to overcome any friction in the mechanism, and ask a companion to look at the clinometer

Figure 54. Using a clinometer to find the angle of elevation of a distant object

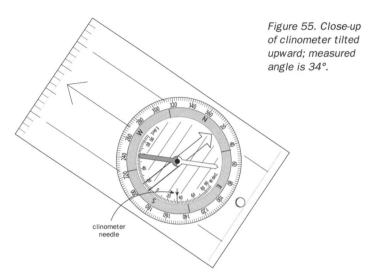

Figure 55. Close-up of clinometer tilted upward; measured angle is 34°.

clinometer needle

needle from the side to see if it indicates an upward or a downward angle toward the other peak. In the close-up of figure 55, the angle is 34°.

> **TIP:** With a mirrored compass, you can read the angle to the object yourself by folding the mirror at a 45° angle, sighting along the edge of the baseplate at the object, and reading the upward or downward angle in the mirror.

If the clinometer indicates an upward angle, then the other peak is higher than you are. (Sorry. You will have to climb that one too.) If you know the elevation angle to any point, such as another peak, then if you read the distance to that point off the map, you can use trigonometry to find the number of feet or meters that the object is higher than you are (elevation above yours = distance x tangent of the elevation angle).

The clinometer can also be used to find the **angle of a slope**. In chapter 6, you learned how to determine the angle of a slope from a map. The clinometer, however, can tell you the actual angle of the slope on which you are standing. As above, set 90° or 270° at the index line, so that it reads zero for the level condition. Then lay the long edge of the compass on the slope (figure 56). Read the angle of the slope on the clinometer scale. Due to variations in the slope over small distances, it is best to place an ice ax, a branch, a trekking pole, or some other long object along the slope, and then place the long edge of the compass along this object to get a better idea of the average slope. The presence of metal, such as an ice ax or trekking pole shaft, will affect the magnetic

Figure 56. Using a clinometer to measure the angle of a given slope at a particular point

needle but not the clinometer needle, which works with gravity (like a plumb bob).

OTHER TYPES OF COMPASSES

Baseplate compasses such as Silva, Suunto, and some others are similar to the models shown in figure 8, and the methods of using these compasses are as described in chapter 2. Several Brunton baseplate compasses, which work differently from those mentioned above, are also available and can be used in wilderness navigation.

Some Brunton compasses have adjustable declination arrows, but there is no screwdriver adjustment as with other compasses. These are referred to as having "tool-free declination adjustment." Instead, these have a round **capsule** within the rotating housing. To adjust for declination, you must squeeze this capsule between your thumb and forefinger while you grasp the rotating housing, or bezel, with your other hand. Then you turn the capsule to point the declination arrow to the correct number of degrees, as shown in figure 57 (for example, 12° E in northwest Utah, or 345° in New Hampshire, for a declination of 15° W). The compass is then used to take and follow bearings in the field in the same way as other compasses described in chapter 2.

Some Brunton compasses, such as the TruArc 3, have no meridian lines in the transparent capsule, so the procedure for measuring and plotting bearings on maps is also slightly different. These compasses have partial meridian lines, aligned with north and south on the dial, on the outer ring of the rotating housing. To measure or plot bearings on a map, follow the procedures described earlier for other compasses,

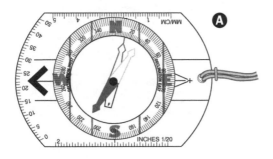

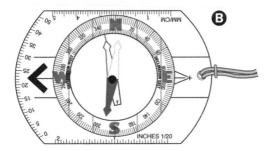

Figure 57.
Adjusting a Brunton
TruArc 3 compass
for declination: A. for
Utah, 12° east and
B. for New Hampshire,
15° west

except **align the partial meridian lines** on the outside ring **with the north–south lines** on the map. As with the other compasses, always make sure that the N on the rotating compass dial is aligned toward north (usually the top) of the map. In figure 58, a Brunton TruArc 3 compass is being used to measure the bearing from point A to point B on a map. The partial meridian lines on the rotating housing are aligned with the meridian lines on the map, and you can see the result (320°) at the index line.

Some Brunton compasses in their newer TruArc series have "On the Map Meridian Lines" like the other baseplate compasses described in chapter 2. These are identified as TruArc models 5, 7, 10, 15, and 20, and they can be used in the same way as the compasses described in chapter 2.

Some baseplate compasses have rotating housings which are marked from 0° to 90° and back to 0°, and then to 90° and back to 0° again. These are called **quadrant** types, and some people prefer them. Bearings taken with a quadrant compass are often expressed as the number of degrees east or west of north or south. For example, S 20° E, which means 20° east of south, or 180° minus 20° equals 160°. We do not recommend these for wilderness navigation, since using them requires the use of mental arithmetic—and you know what we think of *that*.

For wilderness travel we recommend baseplate compasses. All of the examples of taking, following, measuring, and plotting bearings are based on the assumption that you are using such a compass. Most of the compasses listed in chapter 2 are marked to 2° divisions, and it is unlikely that you can achieve better accuracy than that with those compasses. Many people have difficulty obtaining better than 5° accuracy using compasses without a mirror. Even with a mirror, it is difficult to get accuracy consistently better than 2°. If you need better accuracy, there are other, more precise compasses, most notably **optical sighting compasses**, which can provide better accuracy than baseplate compasses.

There are also battery-operated **digital compasses**. Some of these are more accurate and more precise than most baseplate compasses and are useful if the accuracy you need is not possible with a baseplate

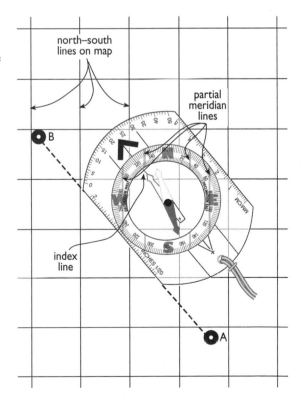

*Figure 58.
Using a Brunton
TruArc 3 compass
to measure a
bearing on a map*

compass. Some wrist-worn **altimeter watches** also contain compasses, such as the "ABC" watches (for altimeter, barometer, and compass). They also tell the time. Some of these have adjustable declination, while others do not, so with some of these you may need to add or subtract declination (as described in chapter 2). Most of these are not baseplate compasses, so in order to use any of these with a map you also need to have a protractor or a baseplate compass to measure and plot bearings.

Another type of **wrist-worn compass** device combines a simple GPS receiver with an "ABC" watch. Some of these are the Garmin Fenix and Forerunner, and the Suunto Ambit (see chapter 9). These are quite expensive, but they allow the user to determine precise position information (such as lat/long or UTM position coordinates) using the GPS feature and to measure and follow compass bearings using the digital compass, while monitoring altitude or barometric pressure with the altimeter/barometer sensor. Some of these have additional features such as heart rate monitors and the ability to record training statistics.

We recommend that if you purchase such a wrist-worn compass, you always bring along a nonelectronic baseplate compass, as well as a paper map, on your wilderness adventures, so that you can use it to measure and plot bearings on a map and to avoid completely depending on an electronic device with limited battery power.

Lensatic compasses are used by the US Army. Detailed instructions for their use are contained in the Army's *Field Manual for Map Reading and Land Navigation*. Lensatic compasses are specially optimized for military purposes and have dials marked in mils as well as in degrees. (There are 6400 mils in a 360-degree circle, or approximately 18 mils to a degree.)

Lensatic compasses are not available with adjustable declination corrections, so the user must mentally add or subtract declination to convert between magnetic and true bearings. Plus, they cannot be used as protractors to measure and plot bearings on a map, so you must carry a separate protractor. For these reasons, we do not recommend lensatic compasses for wilderness navigation, and we focus on baseplate compasses in this book.

If you already have a lensatic compass and are proficient with it, you can use it to navigate in the wilderness. Simply refer to the aforementioned *Field Manual* instead of the instructions in Chapter 2 of this book. However, we encourage you to try to use a baseplate compass so that you may realize its advantages for wilderness navigation.

Baseplate compasses can be found at most outdoor recreation stores, while nautical supply stores usually carry optical sighting compasses. In addition, several mail-order companies sell compasses, altimeters, GPS receivers, and other equipment of interest to the wilderness traveler. One such company is Forestry Suppliers, Inc. (1-800-647-5368; www.forestry-suppliers.com). You can also check out the variety of compasses available at some compass manufacturers' websites, such as www.brunton.com, www.silvacompass.com, and www.suunto.com.

CHAPTER SUMMARY

In this chapter, we explained where to get declination information, as well as why and by how much the magnetic declination is changing. We described what is meant by compass dip, and how to deal with it, as well as the use of the clinometer feature of some compasses. Finally, we discussed some features and uses of compasses of types not covered in chapter 2.

SKILLS CHECK

- Where can you find current declination for your geographic area?
- By how much is declination changing in your geographic area?
- Why is compass dip important? When is it a concern to you?
- List three ways that you can avoid problems with compass dip.
- Describe two different ways that you can use the compass clinometer.
- What is meant by an "ABC" watch?

The Altimeter

CHAPTER OBJECTIVES

- Explain the types and general features of altimeters.
- Describe effects of barometric pressure on altimeter readings.
- Describe the effects of temperature on altimeter readings.
- Explain cautions for using altimeters in wilderness travel.
- Explain the difference between altimeter accuracy and precision, or resolution.
- Explain the use of altimeters in orientation and navigation.
- Show how altimeters can aid in your decision-making.
- Explain the use of altimeters in predicting the weather.
- Show how using the altimeter plus the bearing of the slope can aid in orientation.

An altimeter, like a compass, provides one simple piece of information that forms the basis for a tremendous amount of vital detail: **elevation**. By monitoring the elevation and checking it against the topographic map, wilderness travelers can keep track of their progress, pinpoint their location, and find their way to critical junctions on the route. In mountainous terrain, the altimeter can be a great help in orientation, navigation, and routefinding.

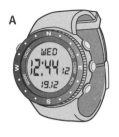

Figure 59. Typical altimeters: A. digital wristwatch; B. digital pocket; C. analog pocket

WHAT AN ALTIMETER IS AND HOW IT WORKS

An altimeter is basically a modified barometer. Both instruments measure air pressure (the weight of air). A **barometer** measures air pressure on a scale calibrated in inches of mercury, millibars, kilopascals, or other units. An **altimeter** also measures air pressure, but its scale is calibrated in feet or meters above or below sea level. This is possible because air pressure changes at a known, predictable rate with changing altitude. The higher the altitude, the lower the air pressure.

TYPES OF ALTIMETERS

The most popular type of wilderness altimeter is the digital wristwatch combination (figure 59A). **Digital pocket altimeters** (figure 59B) are also available. A digital altimeter has several advantages over the analog type (figure 59C). Some digital altimeters display additional information, such as the temperature and the rate of altitude gain or loss. Since most people wear a watch anyway, this type of altimeter is often preferred because it combines multiple functions into one piece of equipment. The altimeter worn on the wrist is also more convenient, and therefore will be consulted more frequently than one kept in a pocket or pack.

A disadvantage of a digital altimeter is that it requires a battery that can become discharged or can become temporarily disconnected due to mechanical shock, or moisture, causing all of its data to be lost (as once happened to one of the authors). The liquid crystal display (LCD) usually goes blank at temperatures near 0°F (−18°C), making it essential to keep the instrument relatively warm. (This is usually not a problem as long as you keep the altimeter on your wrist. If it gets cold enough for the LCD to go blank, the altimeter still retains all of its data and will display the data properly once it warms up enough for the display to work.)

TIP: When starting a technical rock-climbing pitch, it is a good idea to remove your altimeter (or any other jewelry, including rings or bracelets, for that matter) and attach it to your shoulder strap or put it into your pack or pocket to keep it from getting damaged on the rock or stuck in a crack.

There is a very wide range of altimeters available, from simple devices costing as little as $60 to units with a huge array of sophisticated features, and costing up to $600. These generally fall into three categories:

1. **Basic, inexpensive altimeters** (less than $200): These units, mostly digital wristwatch type (though also some analog units), provide a readout of either altitude or barometric pressure, some with a resolution of either 5 meters or 20 feet, though some in this range have resolutions as little as 1 meter or 3 feet. Most units in this price range do not have additional functions such as compasses. Such units are usually adequate for most casual hiking and climbing.

2. **Intermediate-range devices** ($200 to approximately $400): These devices, almost entirely digital wristwatch styles, have all the features of the basic units, but have additional functions such as compasses, cumulative elevation gain and loss, tighter resolution (almost always down to 1 meter or 3 feet), ascent and descent rates, stopwatch functions, countdown timers, and more. These include the popular "ABC" (altimeter, barometer, compass) digital watches.

3. **Top-of-the-line units** ($400 to $600): Some units in this price range, such as the Suunto Ambit and the Garmin Fenix and Forerunner, add a GPS receiver and sometimes a heart-rate monitor to the other altimeter watch features. These units allow their users to identify their point position in either latitude/longitude or UTM coordinates, which can then enable them to find their exact position on a paper map. Though the GPS receivers included in these units are not as complex and versatile as dedicated GPS receivers and smartphones with GPS apps (see chapter 9), they nevertheless can provide very important information to aid in orientation and navigation.

Additional details of these and other such devices are available on the manufacturers' websites such as www.suunto.com, www.casio.com, www .garmin.com, www.rei.com, www.forestrysuppliers.com, and www .thealtimeterstore.com. Be sure to carefully read the characteristics of the altimeter you intend to buy before doing so. Pay particular attention to features such as precision or resolution (the smallest marked or displayed unit of elevation), user-replaceable batteries, etc., as compared with your intended use of the device. For example, rates of ascent and descent may be more important to the hiker than the skier. If you intend to use the device in casual hiking, the most appropriate unit might be a simple, inexpensive wristwatch altimeter that displays the time and the altitude to the nearest five meters, and little else. Furthermore, you might want to consider the type of terrain in which you intend to travel. If you travel in mountainous terrain, an altimeter is a nearly indispensable aid to travel. If you never intend to leave the flatlands, where there are no appreciable elevation changes, any altimeter at all might be a waste of money for you.

The **analog altimeter** has the advantage of being a simpler instrument. It requires no battery and continues to display the elevation even at temperatures well below zero. To read an analog altimeter, hold it level in the palm of your hand. Look directly down on the needle, your eyes at least a foot (30 cm) above it, to reduce errors due to viewing angle (parallax). Tap it lightly several times to overcome any slight friction in the mechanism.

PRECISION AND ACCURACY

Because even the most precise and costly altimeters are strongly influenced by atmospheric conditions, do not be misled into trusting them to a degree of accuracy that is greater than possible. A typical high-quality altimeter may have a resolution, or *precision* (smallest marked division of an analog instrument, or smallest indicated change of a digital one) of 1 meter (3 feet). This does not mean the altimeter will always be that *accurate* (closeness to the truth). Changes in weather could easily throw its reading off by hundreds of feet or meters, even if it is highly precise. This is an important fact to keep in mind when evaluating altimeters. Some of the least-expensive wristwatch altimeters have a resolution of 5 meters (16 feet), which may seem like a lot, but is insignificant for most hiking and climbing situations. Such a unit may be perfectly acceptable for your activities, even though some of your companions may boast that their altimeters are much better than yours because they have a 1-meter resolution. Both will be equally affected by weather-caused barometric pressure variations, which can introduce errors far exceeding the degree of precision.

EFFECTS OF BAROMETRIC PRESSURE ON ALTIMETERS

The accuracy of an altimeter depends on the weather, because a change in the weather is usually accompanied by a change in barometric (air) pressure, which causes an error in the altimeter reading. A change in barometric pressure of 1 inch of mercury corresponds to a change in altitude of roughly 1000 feet. (A pressure change of 10 millibars corresponds to about 100 meters of elevation change.)

Example: If you are in camp during a day in which the air pressure increases by two-tenths of an inch of mercury or 7 millibars (for example, from 30.00 to 30.20 inches, or from 1016 to 1023 millibars), your altimeter will show a reading about 200 feet (60 m) less than it was at the beginning of the day, even though you have remained in the same place. If you had gone out on a hike during that same day, your elevation readings by the end of the day would likewise have been about 200 feet (60 m) too low. During periods of unstable weather, the elevation indicated on your altimeter may change by as much as 500 feet (150 m) in one day even though your actual elevation has remained the same. Even during apparently stable conditions, an erroneous indicated change in elevation of 100 feet (30 m) per day is not uncommon. (Given these errors, what difference does it make whether your altimeter has a resolution of 1 meter or 5 meters?)

EFFECTS OF TEMPERATURE ON ALTIMETERS

The altimeter sensor expands and contracts due to variations in temperature, causing changes in the indicated elevation. A bimetallic element in **temperature-compensated altimeters** adjusts for this effect *when there is no actual change in elevation.* When you are gaining or losing elevation, however, this compensation is often not enough, resulting in errors even in temperature-compensated altimeters.

CAUTIONS WHEN USING AN ALTIMETER

Because of the strong influence of temperature and barometric pressure on an altimeter's accuracy, you cannot trust the instrument until you first **set it at a known elevation**, such as a trailhead. Then it is important, when you are traveling, to **check the reading** whenever you reach other points of known elevation, so you can reset it if necessary, or at least be aware of the error. Get to know your altimeter, use it often, check it at every opportunity, and note differences of opinion between it and the map. You will soon learn just what level of accuracy to expect, and your altimeter will become a dependable aid to roving the wilds.

COPING WITH TEMPERATURE CHANGES

To minimize the effects of temperature changes, try to keep the altimeter's temperature as constant as possible. Body heat will help to accomplish this with a wristwatch altimeter, particularly if it is worn under a parka when the outside temperature is low. With an analog altimeter, you can keep its temperature relatively constant by carrying it in your pocket rather than in your pack.

USING AN ALTIMETER IN WILDERNESS TRAVEL

Knowing your elevation at any time might seem interesting, but you may wonder how you can actually use this information when navigating in the wilderness. The answer is that using an altimeter can be a big help to you in the following ways:

- Orientation (finding your point position)
- Navigation (getting to where you want to go)
- Wise decision-making (e.g., whether to proceed or turn back)
- Predicting the weather
- Enhancing the usefulness of using the bearing of the slope

Orientation

An altimeter can be a big help in determining exactly where you are. If you are climbing a ridge, following a stream uphill, or hiking up a trail shown on the map, but you do not know exactly where you are along the ridge, stream, or trail, check the altimeter for the elevation. Where the ridge, stream, or trail reaches that contour line on the map is your likely location.

Navigation

Navigation becomes easier with an altimeter. For example, if you top a convenient couloir at 9400 feet (2870 meters) and gain the ridge you want to ascend, make a note of that elevation in a notebook or on the map. On your return, descend the ridge to that same elevation and you should easily find the couloir again, even if clouds have come in and obscured all visibility. (This happened to one of the authors on a climb of Mount Shasta.)

Guidebook descriptions sometimes specify a change of direction at a particular elevation. If you are on an open snowfield or a forested hillside, good luck in making the turn at the right place without an altimeter. The route you have worked out on a topographic map also may depend on course changes at certain elevations, and again the altimeter will keep your party on target.

Wise Decision-Making

The altimeter can help you to decide whether to continue a trip or to turn back by letting you calculate your rate of ascent. Suppose you have been keeping an hourly check on time and elevation during a climb. It has taken the party four hours to ascend 3000 feet (910 m), an average of 750 feet (230 m) per hour. But you know that the actual rate of ascent has been declining with each hour. In fact, the party gained only 500 feet (150 m) in the past hour, compared with 1000 feet (300 m) in the first hour. You know that the destination is at an elevation of 8400 feet (2560 m), and an altimeter reading shows you are now at 6400 feet (1950 m).

You can therefore predict that it will take roughly four more hours to reach your destination. Take that information, courtesy of the altimeter, combine it with a look at the weather, the time of the day, and the condition of team members, and you have the data on which to base a sound decision as to whether to proceed with the trip or turn back.

Predicting the Weather

The altimeter can help in predicting the weather. The readings on an **altimeter and a barometer operate in opposition** to one another. When one goes up, the other goes down. An altimeter reading that shows an increase in elevation when no actual elevation change has taken place (such as at camp overnight) means a falling barometer, which often predicts deteriorating weather. An altimeter reading that shows a decrease in elevation, on the other hand, means increasing barometric pressure and possibly improving weather. This is an oversimplification, of course; weather forecasting is complicated by the wind, local weather peculiarities, and the rate of barometric pressure change.

Some digital wristwatch altimeters can be set to read barometric pressure instead of altitude. But keep in mind that changes in barometric

CAUTION IN WEATHER FORECASTING

Professional weather forecasters have far more sophisticated weather instruments than a simple barometer, yet they are frequently very wrong. So don't get overly confident in predicting weather just from altimeter/barometer readings. Make frequent observations of altimeter readings and weather patterns on your trips—and even while at home—if you want to figure out the relationship between weather and altimeter readings in your particular geographic area.

pressure are useful in assessing the weather only when the readings are taken at a constant elevation (such as in camp). Using the altimeter as a barometer while you are ascending or descending will give readings that are influenced not only by changes in barometric pressure but also by changes in your elevation as you travel. Your conclusions about barometric pressure trends may be erroneous under such circumstances.

Use of Bearing of the Slope with an Altimeter

The **bearing of the slope** (described in chapter 3) becomes a very powerful tool when combined with altimeter use. Sometimes, when on a featureless snow slope, in a dense forest, or in foggy conditions, it is impossible to take bearings on visible landmarks, and there are no identifiable topographic features for you to compare to the map. Under these and similar conditions, knowing your altitude plus the bearing of the slope can often provide enough information to enable you to determine your position with a high degree of certainty. In fact, in the absence of definite topographic features or visible landmarks, the use of the altimeter plus the bearing of the slope might well be the *only* way to determine your position, unless you have a GPS device.

Altitude Function in GPS Devices

GPS devices (see chapter 9) provide your position in three dimensions (latitude and longitude [or UTM] and altitude) using satellites instead of barometric pressure sensors. They are therefore not subject to errors due to changing temperatures or atmospheric conditions, and usually indicate your elevation to the nearest foot or meter, which means they can be used instead of the pressure sensor altimeters described above. But there are disadvantages to relying on them for altitude information.

First, the batteries in digital altimeters have a lifetime usually measured in months or years, and analog altimeters do not depend on batteries, whereas those in dedicated GPS receivers and in smartphones with GPS apps are limited to hours or days. Secondly, though GPS-indicated altitude has a resolution of one foot or one meter, their altitude accuracy is not as good as their ground position accuracy, and can have an error of 100 feet (about 30 meters) or even more. Also, digital and analog altimeters continuously display altitude, always available at a glance, whereas GPS devices require some time to acquire a valid position after being powered up. For these reasons, many mountain travelers choose to use a digital wristwatch or analog altimeter, even if they are also using a GPS device.

CHAPTER SUMMARY

This chapter has covered different types and characteristics of altimeters, what they do and how they work, and the important distinction between resolution (precision) and accuracy. Some important suggestions were given explaining how to make the best use of altimeters, and we explained how to use an altimeter in orientation, navigation, decision-making, predicting weather, and determining the bearing of the slope.

SKILLS CHECK

- What are two advantages of analog altimeters over digital ones?
- What are two advantages of digital altimeters over analog ones?
- What is the difference between precision (resolution) and accuracy?
- How do we correct for altimeter inaccuracies because of changing weather conditions?
- Does a temperature-compensated altimeter always compensate for temperature? Why?
- Briefly describe two examples of how you can use an altimeter in the process of orientation.
- How can an altimeter be used in weather prediction?

PRACTICE PROBLEMS *See the appendix for problem instructions.*

- Problems 21 and 27 involve orientation using a map and altimeter readings.

The Global Positioning System

Note: If you skipped all the other chapters and turned to this one first, thinking that using the Global Positioning System (GPS) will make it unnecessary for you to learn how to use a map and compass, please **go back to the beginning** of the book and read at least chapters 1 through 6 before reading this chapter. Using GPS technology most effectively requires a basic understanding of how to read maps and how to use a compass.

CHAPTER OBJECTIVES

- Explain the Global Positioning System.
- Provide advice on selecting a GPS device.
- Explain how to get started with GPS.
- Explain how to use GPS in the wilderness.
- Explain how to use a GPS receiver with a computer.
- Discuss using GPS functions with smartphones.
- Explain limitations of GPS receivers.
- Show how to cope with limitations of GPS technology.

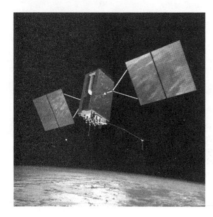

Figure 60.
Typical GPS satellite
(Courtesy of www.gps.gov)

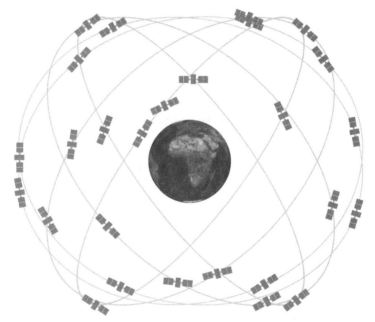

Figure 61. GPS satellites in orbit around Earth (Courtesy of www.gps.gov)

In this chapter, the term "GPS receiver" refers to dedicated GPS devices, such as those made by Garmin and Magellan. The GPS can also be accessed by smartphones with GPS apps installed. The term "GPS devices" refers to all devices capable of receiving and utilizing GPS signals. The use of smartphones with GPS apps is explained later in this chapter.

The US Department of Defense has placed a system of twenty-eight satellites (plus a few spares; see figure 60) in orbit around Earth (see figure 61). Some other countries have also created similar systems, such as Russia's GLONASS, or have plans to do so in the future. GPS devices pick up signals from some of these satellites and can give the user's geographic position and altitude to within about 50 feet (15 meters) under ideal conditions.

The unique utility of a GPS device is that it can give you your position on Earth's surface (to within a sphere with a radius about the size of a racquetball court) and, in addition, can tell you the distance and direction to any other known position. In other words, it can provide you precise orientation and navigation, in the absence of any visible landmarks. This development has revolutionized navigation.

SELECTING A GPS RECEIVER

Most dedicated GPS receivers cost from $100 to $600 and have a variety of features that allow them to store and later recall specific positions (called **waypoints**) and plot out routes comprising a series of waypoints from one position to another. The difference between the inexpensive units and the expensive ones is generally in the number of additional features that they have.

There are some very inexpensive units (under $100) that only tell you how to *get back* to a previously saved waypoint. Examples are the Bushnell BackTrack (see figure 62) and the Brunton GET-BACK. Though they do not display your actual position coordinates and cannot guide you to a waypoint you have not previously visited, they can nevertheless be used in an emergency to avoid getting totally lost, by pointing out the distance and direction to one of a few previously visited and saved waypoints (such as car, camp, and home). They are the simplest of all GPS units to learn how to use. You might consider such a unit if you intend to use it only for emergency backup.

Figure 62. Bushnell BackTrack GPS receiver

A big step up from these are the slightly more expensive ($100 to $150) units that display the lat/long or UTM coordinates (explained in chapter 6) of hundreds or even thousands of waypoints. Examples are the Garmin eTrex 10 and Foretrex 301 and the Magellan eXplorist 110. They do not display your position on a map, but by reading your UTM or lat/long coordinates on the unit's screen, you can find your position on the paper topo map or chart that you still must carry. These units also allow you to enter the UTM or lat/long coordinates of places where you have never visited, by finding these coordinates from your paper map and entering these into the GPS unit. Most of these units do not include compasses, so you still need to use your baseplate compass to point you in the right direction to your destination.

Figure 63. Garmin eTrex 20 GPS device

More expensive models ($150 to $300) also display their locations on detailed digital topographical maps or charts. Examples are the Magellan eXplorist 310 and 510 and the Garmin eTrex 20 (figure 63) and eTrex 30. These come with a preloaded "base map" that contains major roads and highways, but no detailed maps with topographic features. The latter can be added by purchasing separate digital maps on cards that usually cost $80 to $100 for a state or region.

The most expensive receivers ($300 to $600) add preloaded topographic maps, compasses, cameras, touch screens, and/or wireless communication. Examples include the Magellan eXplorist 610 (figure 64) and 710,

Figure 64. Magellan eXplorist 610 GPS device

Figure 65. DeLorme Earthmate
PN-60W GPS device

Garmin Oregon 550t, Montana 600, and DeLorme Earthmate PN-60 and PN-60W (figure 65). Also in this group are GPS-enabled "ABC" (altimeter, barometer, compass) sport wristwatches such as the Suunto Ambit (figure 66) and Garmin Fenix and Forerunner.

There is no need to spend a lot of money for a GPS device with pre-loaded topo maps, a touch screen, a built-in compass, a camera, and other refinements. A basic device costing less than $150 will perform all the essential GPS functions you need for orientation and navigation, though you must use it together with your paper map and baseplate compass, which you must still carry with you anyway.

Some receivers are designed to make use of additional satellites that comprise the Wide Area Augmentation System (WAAS) in the United States, resulting in even greater accuracy—as close as 3 meters (10 feet) under ideal conditions, if you have an adequate view of the southern sky. Such receivers are said to be "WAAS enabled." Similar systems, such as the European Geostationary Navigation Overlay Service (EGNOS) and Japan's Multi-functional Satellite Augmentation System (MSAS) also exist, and more are planned for other areas. Some device manufacturers refer to such systems as Space-Based Augmentation Systems (SBAS). These systems were designed primarily for aviation purposes, to aid in flight control and air-craft landing. Their usefulness in ground applications such as wilderness navigation is limited by the fact that such satellites appear very close to the horizon from northern areas, since the satellites are in orbit over the

Figure 66. Suunto Ambit GPS watch

earth's equator. This limits their effectiveness in the northern United States, Canada, and northern Europe and Asia.

Much useful information on GPS receivers is available on manufacturers' websites such as www.magellangps.com, www.garmin.com, and the US government GPS website, www.gps.gov.

GETTING STARTED WITH GPS

Avoid the temptation to rush out into the wilderness, get lost, and trust that this marvelous electronic gadget will magically get you home again. Instead, at least read its Quick Start Guide, a shorter and abbreviated version of the instruction manual. (This chapter is intended only as a supplement to the instruction manual that comes with your GPS receiver.)

Select which units to use (miles or kilometers, feet or meters, magnetic or true bearings, etc.) and—very important—select the **datum to agree with the topographic map** of the area (the datum was explained in chapter 6). These options are generally accessible using the device's "Settings" or "Set Up" function. If you are using the compass methods described in chapter 2 of this book, be sure to use **true bearings** (usually the default north reference setting) rather than magnetic bearings. Try out the receiver around your home, in city parks, and on easy trail hikes before taking it into the wilderness. Eventually, read the entire instruction manual to learn of all its features.

The most important rule of using a GPS receiver is to avoid becoming dependent on it. It is best to consider the GPS receiver as an extra navigational tool, as a useful addition to a paper map and a magnetic compass, rather than as a replacement for them. If conditions warrant, carry route-marking materials such as flagging and wands, regardless of whether or not you have a GPS receiver. **Never rely solely on a GPS receiver for navigation.**

USING A GPS RECEIVER IN WILDERNESS NAVIGATION

To minimize battery usage, you can use your GPS receiver along with a map and compass in order to ensure that you can get back to your starting point. For example, at the trailhead or campsite, or wherever you start your trip, turn the receiver on to establish your GPS position. Compare the displayed coordinates to the map to ensure that it makes sense. (Under rare but nevertheless occasional conditions, erroneous positions are sometimes displayed.) If the position looks valid, save this position as a waypoint, even giving it a unique name (such as CAR or CAMP) if desired. Then turn off the receiver to save battery power, and pack it away carefully to protect it from harm while you are traveling. Along the route, you may encounter crucial locations, such as important trail junctions, the point where you reach a trail or a ridge crest, etc. At such points, turn on the receiver to establish additional waypoints. Again, make sure their coordinates match those on the map. Once you are at your destination or turnaround point, use the receiver to find the distance and compass bearing from one waypoint to another to return to the starting point. Then turn off the receiver and follow a trail or topography, or use your compass to travel to the next waypoint. At any point at which you turn on the receiver and get a position, you can ask the receiver to GO to any previously stored waypoint. The receiver will then provide the distance and compass bearing to that waypoint.

Many GPS instruction manuals seem to assume that you are always traveling with the receiver turned on and in your hand, constantly observing its display. Doing this wastes battery power and occupies a hand that might be better used for climbing, scrambling, or holding an ice ax or a trekking pole. In addition, it distracts you from observing the route, its hazards, and the scenery, and it looks really nerdy. The most efficient way to use GPS is to **use it only occasionally** and to travel by map and compass the rest of the time.

Under some conditions it might be advantageous to leave a GPS receiver turned on continuously while you travel—such as when you are descending through the forest, down a snow slope in a whiteout, or when it is late and darkness is approaching. Under such conditions, every minute might count, making it inconvenient to stop for a few minutes every now and then to turn the receiver on and then allow it to reacquire the position.

If you decide to leave your receiver on as you travel toward your destination, it will record your route. Then on your return trip you can use the receiver's **backtrack** mode to retrace your steps very closely. This feature can only be used if you leave the receiver on the entire time en route to your destination, as well as on the return trip. Obviously, this method will exhaust batteries much more quickly than occasional use, so carrying spare batteries is essential.

> **TIP:** If you want to leave the receiver turned on so that you can refer to it continuously, we suggest that you find a way to securely attach it to a pack strap or some other easily accessible place so your hands are free while you travel. Then you can look at the receiver any time you want while using your hands for other purposes.

Be sure to start each wilderness adventure with a fresh set of batteries, and consider carrying spares, depending on the length of your projected trip and your estimated usage of the device.

GPS receivers have some obvious advantages over magnetic compasses. A compass can tell you your position only if you can see landmarks and can take bearings on them. The GPS receiver, on the other hand, can provide your position **without any visible landmarks** (under ideal conditions). This can be particularly helpful in fog or a whiteout or in featureless terrain.

In chapter 4 we described various strategies to use to follow a compass bearing toward your objective, such as the use of intermediate objectives and detouring around an obstruction. When using a compass, such techniques are essential in order to stay on your correct course. With a GPS receiver, however, navigation becomes easier. If you are trying to follow a given bearing to your destination and the route is blocked, you can simply travel around the blockage by the easiest route without worrying about how far off route you get or in what direction. Once past the obstruction, you can again turn on your GPS receiver, obtain a new position, and the receiver will provide the new bearing to your objective. Then you can set that new bearing on your compass and follow it.

> **TIP:** When planning a wilderness trip, we suggest that you find the coordinates of critical sites (e.g., the starting point, critical junctions, the destination, and other crucial points) on the map and enter them into the GPS receiver as waypoints. This is easiest to do at home before your trip.

INTERFACING A GPS RECEIVER WITH A HOME COMPUTER

The GPS device on its own is a great tool, but when you connect it to your home computer a whole new world of functionality emerges. If you are a Mac user, be sure that the GPS device you buy is compatible with the Mac OS operating system. (Almost all GPS devices by default work with the PC Windows operating system if they have computer connectivity at all. Some work only with the Windows operating system.)

> **TIP:** The GPS receiver itself is a valuable navigational tool. It is not absolutely necessary to interface your GPS device with a computer to use it effectively, so you should not feel intimidated by PC interfacing if you are not proficient with computer usage.

Internet and Physical Connections

If you seek PC compatibility, internet access is a must, especially if you wish to download plug-ins, additional software, and updates. A physical connection between your GPS receiver and computer (PC) is necessary for the two to communicate, usually through a USB cable, though sometimes via wireless connectivity. Follow the receiver's instructions on how to make such a connection.

Software Upgrade

Once the GPS device is recognized by your home computer, it is possible that the device will need a software upgrade. If so, follow the onscreen directions to do so. If there is no paper user's manual, then you may have to download it from the internet.

Removable Memory

Many GPS receivers have a slot (sometimes hidden behind the batteries) to accept portable memory on an SD or micro-SD card (see figure 67). This is used to transfer maps and to use as expandable memory for screenshots and photographs (if so equipped). This enables you to map out an entire trip on the large-screen monitor of your home computer and save that trip and all its waypoints to the memory card.

Figure 67. Micro-SD card compared to a dime

Trip Planning and Analysis

Once you have established communication between your GPS device and your home computer, you have the ability to define waypoints and routes on your PC, and then to transfer them to the GPS receiver, either directly though the cable, or by entering the lat/long or UTM coordinates directly into the receiver manually.

Using the GPS unit and home computer interface also allows you to analyze a trip once completed. On your trip you may have collected data via your GPS device, such as your starting point, waypoints, tracks, and other GPS data. Once you return home, your device (or SD card) can be connected to your home computer to analyze the data, or to share it with friends. You can often display your rate of elevation gain, speed of travel, distance traveled, and other information.

Brand-Specific Software

The websites for the receivers (e.g., www.garmin.com, www.magellangps .com, etc.) usually have instructions for loading the brand-specific software onto your computer. Garmin uses Garmin Connect Base Camp, and Magellan uses Vantage Point. All of these are included with the purchase of these three brands, though for Garmin units, the actual 1:24,000-scale topo maps for each geographic area are available on SD cards at added cost. Some GPS device instruction manuals have only limited information on how to use these software packages. In these cases, finding and reading on-screen "help" instructions will enable you to find how to perform these functions.

LIMITATIONS AND PITFALLS OF GPS RECEIVERS

The GPS receiver is not a substitute for a map and compass or the ability to use them. **Many GPS receivers cannot determine direction**, so you still need a compass to use GPS in the wilderness. Most GPS receivers can tell you the straight-line route from one point to another, but they have no way of knowing if there is a river, a lake, or a cliff along this route. For this reason, you still must have a topographic map with you, even if you also have a GPS receiver.

The more expensive GPS receivers contain built-in maps and can accept topographic maps downloaded from your computer. These receivers can show your position directly on the screen of your receiver. While this is a very useful feature, it **does not replace the need for conventional paper maps**, because you still need to be able to view the big picture of the route as well as to avoid total dependence on the GPS receiver. Furthermore, using the electronic maps requires a great deal of panning and zooming in and out, which can be tedious and time- and power-consuming. It is easier and quicker to simply glance at a paper topo map.

Some GPS receivers also contain built-in electronic compasses. Using such an instrument eliminates the need to set the correct course bearing on your magnetic compass. You could then conceivably do all your navigating using only your GPS receiver. Even with such a receiver, however, you **still need to carry a magnetic compass**, in case the GPS receiver's compass loses its calibration (which can happen when the batteries are replaced, or if the device is dropped or bumped, or sometimes for no apparent reason), exhausts its batteries, or otherwise fails to work properly.

Most GPS receivers will not work at temperatures much below freezing, and battery life is limited to fifteen to thirty hours, depending on the model and the type of batteries used.

GPS receivers must track signals from at least four satellites in order to provide trustworthy position information, but if the satellite signals are blocked by heavy forest cover, cliffs, or canyons, this is often not possible. When a GPS receiver is not able to pick up signals from four satellites, it sacrifices altitude information in favor of horizontal position. Some receivers indicate that this is happening by displaying a "2D" message or icon to tell you that it is operating in a two-dimensional mode. Some receivers merely display a "frozen" altitude display if this occurs. In either case, always **note whether you are getting a two-dimensional position**. If so, then be aware of the fact that the GPS receiver's horizontal position may be significantly in error as well, particularly if you are thousands of feet or meters above sea level. Under such less-than-ideal conditions, horizontal position errors of 1000 feet (hundreds of meters) or more are possible.

Because of the slight possibility that a GPS receiver might have a position error, it is wise to exercise some caution before using or saving a waypoint. For example, suppose you are in a parking lot at a trailhead and you acquire a GPS position. This will be an important waypoint, since you will certainly want to get back to your vehicle at the end of your trek. Instead of just mindlessly saving this position, you should **first observe the coordinates** indicated on the screen of the receiver and **compare them to the map**. These coordinates should

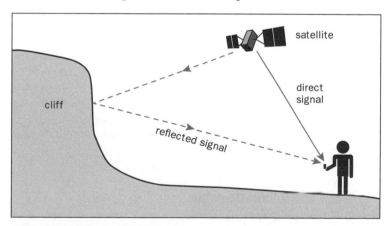

Figure 68. Multipath signal reflection

indicate a position very close to your known location. Also, **observe the elevation** indicated on the GPS receiver screen, and compare it with that shown on your map or altimeter. Again, they should agree closely. Any significant difference between either your known position or altitude and that shown on the GPS receiver should alert you to the possibility that you might have an erroneous GPS position, perhaps due to signal reflections off cliffs, cars, or other structures (see figure 68), or perhaps due to some atmospheric disturbance. In this case, wait a few minutes or walk a short distance and try again. Do not save any important waypoint until you have **verified that it is in reasonable agreement with your position** as shown on the map.

COPING WITH THE LIMITATIONS OF GPS RECEIVERS

A variety of conditions and situations can occur that might prevent the GPS from giving you the information you need for navigation in the wilderness. We have previously mentioned some of these: deep canyons or heavy forest cover that prevent acquisition of enough satellite signals to obtain a position; outside temperatures below the minimum required for the receiver's LCD display; large inaccuracies caused by multipath signals due to reflections of satellite signals; exceeding battery life; losing or damaging your receiver; and electronic failure. These conditions are generally rare, and in many cases preventable. Still, such conditions can and do occur. Although it is impossible to counteract all possible failures and inaccuracies, with a little forethought and planning it should be possible to get to your objective and back home safely even without a functioning GPS receiver.

One obvious preventive measure, particularly when traveling in a group, is to **carry two or more GPS receivers**. These devices are becoming more and more popular and affordable, and when planning a wilderness trip it is often easy to find at least one other person in the party who also has a GPS receiver. The random failure of one receiver could therefore be overcome, but it might not help if the loss of usage is due to a problem affecting both receivers, such as extreme cold, deep canyons, or excessive forest cover. If your navigation plan involves using GPS as your primary navigational tool, you should seriously consider carrying a second receiver on your trip.

Cold-Temperature Operation

Every GPS receiver has a lower-temperature operating limit, below which it will not display any data, due to inherent characteristics of its display. Various receivers have different temperature requirements, but generally this lower limit is somewhere between -5°F and +14°F (-20°C and -10°C), depending on the particular unit. You can usually find this information in the Specifications section of the user manual. If you contemplate using the receiver in such conditions, you should **test the receiver's cold-temperature operation** at or near your home in cold conditions (such as in your freezer) before you trust it to operate in a cold climate. If you need it to operate at a temperature lower than its lower limit, you might resort to carrying it close to your body, in a pocket or other location under several layers of clothing. Most receivers are not permanently damaged due to exposure to cold temperatures, and many still operate and can track your position under cold conditions but simply cannot display your position. They usually return to normal operation after they warm up.

Maximizing Battery Life

Many GPS users complain that their receivers use batteries at a faster rate than advertised. There are a few things that you can do in order to increase battery life. In many cases you can use longer-lasting **lithium batteries** rather than standard alkaline batteries. Lithium cells cost more but may save you money in the long run since they last longer. Furthermore, they work more reliably at cold temperatures and weigh less.

If you operate your GPS receiver at a **moderate temperature**, its batteries will last longer. You should keep the receiver and any spare batteries out of direct sunlight, and inside your jacket on cold days.

Turn off your receiver when navigation is easy or straightforward, such as while walking along a good, well-maintained trail, as well as when in heavy forest cover or in a canyon where the unit will waste power trying to search for signals that it cannot receive. **Disable the WAAS, EGNOS, or SBAS function** if you do not have a clear view of the horizon, since it takes extra battery power for the receiver to keep searching for a satellite that it cannot find. Some receivers have WAAS permanently enabled, so this may not be an option. See figure 69 for an example of DeLorme's Earthmate: Go to Settings, then System, press ENTER, and choose WAAS on or off. Garmin's eTrex (figure 70) is similar: from the Main Menu, go to Setup, then System, and observe the Satellite System screen. You can then turn WAAS/EGNOS on or off. For the Magellan eXplorist, from the main menu go to Tools, then Satellite, then Options. You should see a screen similar to that in figure 71, allowing you to enable or disable SBAS (Space-Based Augmentation System: the combination of WAAS and EGNOS). Other units made by the same manufacturers have similar ways to turn WAAS off.

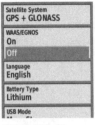

Figure 69. WAAS off on the DeLorme Earthmate PN-60W receiver.

Figure 70. Disable WAAS and EGNOS on the Garmin eTrex 20 receiver.

Figure 71. Disable SBAS on the Magellan eXplorist 610 device.

Additional battery-saving techniques include **reducing backlight brightness and the "timer off" period** for the display screen's light dimmer. Most receivers allow you to set the brightness and timer-off time to lesser values than the default conditions. Also, **disable power drainers** such as the compass, barometer, and altimeter if they are not being used.

Conventional Map-and-Compass Navigation

Of course, the most important method of coping with any GPS problem is your ability to fall back on conventional map and compass navigational techniques. We have warned you against becoming totally dependent on your GPS receiver. **Always carry a compass and a paper topographic map** of the area in which you are traveling, even if the receiver has an electronic compass and a digital map of the area. You should never allow yourself to get into a situation where the failure of an electronic device will jeopardize your safety or your ability to get back home. (Don't ever have to say, "It's not my fault that we got lost—the batteries in my GPS died.")

USING THE GPS FUNCTION IN SMARTPHONES

For many of us, smart phones have become an integral part of our modern world. This section explains how to best use such devices for navigation in the wilderness environment. (In this section we will refer to smart phones and smart devices interchangeably.)

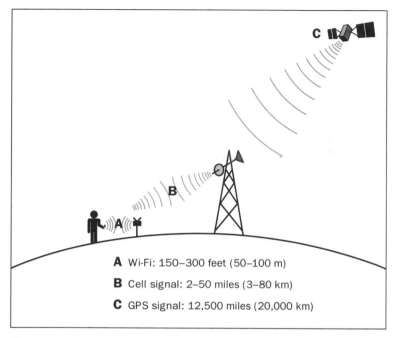

A Wi-Fi: 150–300 feet (50–100 m)

B Cell signal: 2–50 miles (3–80 km)

C GPS signal: 12,500 miles (20,000 km)

Figure 72. Comparative signal ranges of smart devices

Smart phones receive signals from three sources: a Wi-Fi network, the cellular network, and GPS satellites. The ranges of these signals are several hundred feet for Wi-Fi signals and a few miles (up to 50) for cellular phone signals. GPS signals, on the other hand, can travel thousands of miles and are available anywhere on Earth. Figure 72 shows the relative ranges of the three types of signals. In wilderness travel you are often traveling outside of Wi-Fi and cell phone range and are using GPS signals alone.

The GPS Signal, Wi-Fi, and the Cellular Network

Most smart phones have GPS capability. They can display your position on a digital map (see figure 73). However, topographic maps are not transmitted to your device through the GPS satellite signal. The **maps are best downloaded** through the Wi-Fi connection, if one is available; if not, then through the much slower cellular network, neither of which is always available in the wilderness. If you have not downloaded the maps for the area in which you will be traveling, and you are out of Wi-Fi and cell tower range, your smart phone/mobile device may be able to display your position from the GPS signals, but only as a dot on a

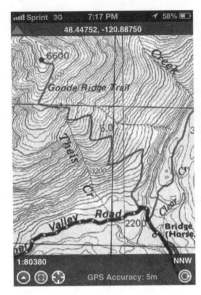
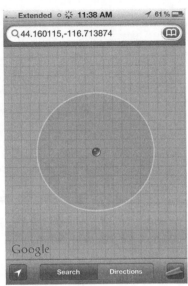

Figure 73. Topo map displayed on an iPhone screen with latitude and longitude coordinates shown at the top of the screen

Figure 74. Position from a GPS signal when out of cell network range

grid or a blank screen (see figure 74). To avoid this, you must **"cache" a map of the area** by panning and zooming into an area that you will be traveling to beforehand, while still in range of Wi-Fi or cell phone towers. We encourage you to load maps of your entire route, plus those of the surrounding area.

If you have not previously downloaded or cached a map of the area and just get a dot on a grid, you should still be able to find your location by getting the device to display the **latitude/longitude** (at the top of figure 74) **or UTM coordinates** even if the map is not displayed. Then you can find your position on the paper map that you will be carrying anyway. But you must always examine these coordinates carefully and make sure that they make sense to you, and that they are not merely the last known coordinates (a common default condition of smart phones as well as dedicated GPS receivers when the device cannot obtain a current satellite position fix).

Alternatively, your smart device may simply tell you that you are "outside of the cellular network" or "Search Results Not Available" (figure 75), politely telling you that it is only receiving half of the data:

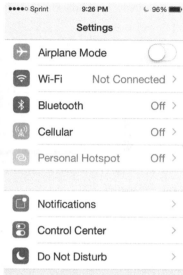

Figure 75. Out-of-cellular-range message displayed on iPhone screen

Figure 76. The Settings screen enables you to turn Wi-Fi, cellular access, and other functions on or off.

position only, without map data. Without a paper map, the coordinates are usually useless for navigation.

There's an App for That!

To **test your smart phone's GPS function**, install one of the many GPS apps, such as Where Am I At?, Green Trails Maps, SkiTracks, AllTrails, Google Maps, Gaia, Backcountry Navigator Pro, or others. Then go into your smart device's settings (see figure 76), with GPS (sometimes described as Location Services) enabled, and simulate the wilderness environment signal reception by turning off your Wi-Fi and cellular network access and by switching to airplane mode. This leaves only the GPS radio waves receivable. Start your GPS app and see what happens. Does it indicate a strong GPS signal? Does it give a location that makes sense to you? Does it give a location at all? If so, make note of it or take a screenshot. To ensure a good position, be sure to observe the displayed position for a few minutes.

Now it's time for a short walk, drive, or bike ride to a familiar location. Leave the Wi-Fi and cellular network off while doing so.

Once you are some distance from where you first obtained a GPS signal, fire up the GPS app and observe the GPS coordinates once again. Compare the new coordinates to the saved screenshot. Are they different? Do the new coordinates match your known position? Oftentimes a GPS device, even a smart device, will display the last known position if a current position cannot be calculated. This is why it is so important to **compare the position** that the device indicates with your known position. Bad information is worse than no information at all. If the new position agrees with your current position, then you have data that you can work with. Experiment with free apps and read reviews of paid apps to see if a particular app is worth the money for your particular needs.

Digital Maps

The key to successful navigation with a smart device is **downloading the most detailed maps** of the area in which you will be traveling **well before your journey begins**. There are several free and paid apps that allow you to download detailed topo maps. Be sure to do this in a civilized area with a strong Wi-Fi signal, since attempting to download detailed maps while driving to remote trailheads can be slow and frustrating, if possible at all. Downloading the map may be as simple as zooming in as close as possible to your entire wilderness route. Your smart device should be capable enough to cache the map data and display it later once it is outside of the cellular network.

PRECAUTIONS WHEN USING SMART MOBILE DEVICES FOR WILDERNESS NAVIGATION

A smart device is an excellent SMS (text messaging) device, a quality phone, an okay camera, a fairly good web surfer, a good portable media player, a good email device, flashlight, MP3 player, and, under perfect conditions, a reliable GPS device. But there is one important drawback to consider: battery life.

Battery Life

Smart device users often complain about the limited battery life of their devices in urban areas, where there is easy access to wall or car chargers. But powering up your GPS receiver on some mobile devices can drain your battery dry within a few hours. This all-in-one device, with limited battery power remaining, will then give you only fleeting access to GPS, Wi-Fi, cell phone, photography, and SMS.

There are, however, a few tips for extending your smart phone's battery life while the GPS function is powered up. The first is to **turn off power-hungry apps**. To further save battery power, turn off all apps that are in your notification center. This will prevent the device from waking up when that particular app is activated by an incoming message, a social media update, stock report, or traffic or news update.

Another useful trick is to **turn down the brightness of the display**, and to decrease the amount of time that the auto-lock feature allows before automatically putting the device into sleep mode. The display consumes much energy, and even a slight dimming will correlate to increased battery life. (That said, on a bright day above tree line, the dimmed display is harder to read.) Experiment with different settings for screen brightness to see just how bright the screen really needs to be in order to be usefully visible outdoors.

Among the plethora of other ways to conserve power for your smart phone (search the internet for your particular device), the best way, of course, is to **turn off your device completely when you don't need it**. Then turn it on only at **key locations**, obtain a good position that agrees with your known position, save the waypoint, and turn it off. In this way the device is only used in necessary routefinding situations.

Limitations of GPS Usage with Smart Devices

The fundamental message here is that if you are accustomed to using your smart device in the city, within cell tower range, and with ample access to power, you cannot be afforded such luxuries in the wilderness, where a different mindset is required.

Supplemental power sources exist for smart devices in the backcountry, including external battery packs, integrated smart device protectors/supplemental battery accessories, electricity-generating stoves, and solar chargers. But how much extra weight are you willing to carry? How will you attach and arrange a solar panel array on your backpack to charge your smart device? Will it be effective as you hike through a dense forest?

PLBS AND SATELLITE COMMUNICATORS

Personal locator beacons (PLBs) determine a party's coordinates using GPS and can transmit them through government satellites to appropriate emergency responders. This communication can initiate a search-and-rescue operation, possibly saving your life. Registration is required, but there are no subscription fees for PLBs using the government-based system.

Two commercial companies have introduced other devices similar to PLBs known as satellite communicators. The ones currently available are the SPOT Satellite GPS Messenger, which allows one-way messaging, and the Garmin inReach Satellite Communicator, which allows two-way messaging. These devices determine your position using GPS and then send a message using commercial satellite networks. Some units allow for short, preset, nonemergency text messages (for example, "Camping here tonight"); some allow users to send free-form text messages; and some allow two-way texting. Satellite communicators require paid subscriptions, and the cost of each manufacturer's plans varies based on factors such as the number of messages transmitted and other services. PLBs and satellite communicators have helped save many lives, and wilderness travelers should strongly consider carrying one to increase their margin of safety.

CHAPTER SUMMARY

GPS receivers are marvelous devices, and using them can significantly aid wilderness navigation. Keep in mind, however, that they are not foolproof, and that topography, forest cover, battery life, electronic failure, cold temperatures, and inadequate user knowledge can prevent their effective use. A GPS receiver cannot replace conventional map and compass techniques. Conventional paper maps and baseplate compasses work at temperatures well below zero, require no batteries, and are so simple that there is very little that can go wrong with them. In addition, compasses are so lightweight and inexpensive that every party member can carry one. They are easy to operate and understand, and they function in even the thickest of forests. GPS devices can be extremely helpful in wilderness navigation, but the map and compass remain the cornerstones of navigation and wilderness routefinding.

SKILLS CHECK

- Does a GPS device replace the need for a topo map?
- Does a GPS device replace the need for a compass?
- Is the GPS (or location services) app on smart phones just as good as a dedicated GPS receiver?

- When using a basic GPS receiver that does not display topo maps, how can you determine your exact position?
- What do WAAS, EGNOS, and SBAS have in common?
- List three things you can do to increase battery life in GPS receivers.

Wilderness Routefinding

CHAPTER OBJECTIVES

- Learn how to properly prepare for trips in the wilderness.
- Explain the importance of having an agreed-upon turnaround time.
- Learn how to routefind on the trail, in the forest, in the desert, in alpine areas, and on snow and glaciers.
- Explain how careful identification of bootprints can aid in wilderness routefinding.
- Describe the art of wilderness routefinding.

TRIP PLANNING AND PREPARATION

Routefinding begins at home. Before heading out the door, you need to know not only the name of your wilderness destination but also a great deal about how to get there and back. This information is accessible to anyone who takes the time to seek it out, from guidebooks, maps, digital sources, and from people who have been there.

Any off-trail trip requires a **route plan**, that is, a well-thought-out procedure for how you will navigate to your destination and back. This includes identifying handrails that you will be following, baselines or catch lines that you could head to in the event of an emergency (see chapter 5), route-marking materials, compass bearings that you might need to follow, GPS coordinates of waypoints of crucial locations, download maps and routes, and any other navigational aids.

Up-to-date guidebooks provide **critical information** such as a description of the route, the estimated time necessary to complete it, elevation gain, distance, and so forth. Travelers who have previously made the trip may be able to tell you about landmarks, hazards, and routefinding hassles. Useful details are packed into maps of all sorts: Forest Service, road, aerial, sketch, and topographic. For a trip into an area that is particularly unfamiliar to you, more preparation is needed. This might include scouting into the area, observations from distant vantage points, or a study of aerial photographs or satellite imagery.

If the route comes from a guidebook or from a description provided by another person or a website, **plot it out** on the topographic map you will be carrying, noting trail junctions and other important points. It can help to highlight the route with a yellow felt-tip marking pen, which does not obliterate map features. Additional maps or route descriptions marked with notes about any more up-to-date information should be taken, along with the topo map. In selecting the route, consider a host of factors including the season, weather and route conditions, the abilities of party members, and the equipment available.

You should not let outdated information ruin your trip. **Check beforehand with the appropriate agencies** about roads and trails, especially closures, and also about off-trail routes, regulations, permits, and camping requirements.

Turnaround Time

Every wilderness adventure, however simple or sublime, must have a predetermined **agreed-upon turnaround time**. This is the time of day when the party must turn around in order to return to the trailhead, camp, or other planned destination before dark. Everyone in your group should know this time and agree to it. Your objective plays an important role in the determination of this time. For example, if your destination is a car parked at a trailhead above tree line, then you have an extra half hour to work with since it will still be light for about a half hour after sunset. However, if your destination is a campsite that you must set up in a thick forest, then you need to be more conservative. Visible light in a thick forest can dim about a half hour *before* sunset. Furthermore, you will need time to set up camp, purify water, prepare dinner, and plan the route for the next day.

Turnaround time should be based on the **amount of available light** during the day. In order to determine your safe turnaround time, first find the time of sunset. Then figure out how long you think it will take for you to get from your objective to the trailhead or camp. Add in an hour or two for lunch breaks and rest stops. On a steep climb, a good general rule is that it will take half the time to descend as it took to ascend the same route. For a level route, a nearly equal time may be required. Add the descent time to your anticipated ascent time and add in an hour or so for unplanned emergencies. For example, suppose you plan on a four-hour ascent time with two hours of descent time, on a day when the sun rises at 8 a.m. and sets at 6 p.m. With an extra hour for good measure, this puts your turnaround time at 3 p.m. at the latest. With more experience you will learn the capabilities of your team members, but it is wise to start out conservatively for maximum safety.

On a typical glacier or snow climb, your turnaround time may be as early as 10 a.m. to avoid soft snow conditions on the descent. This often entails a predawn start. If the ascent is expected to require eight hours, with four hours of descent time, you may want to return to camp by noon, which would necessitate a midnight start time.

Return Route

As a general rule, it is best to return from your objective by means of the **same route** that you take to your objective. If so, you will be knowledgeable about route conditions, trail junctions, and any potential routefinding pitfalls. That said, however, there are times when you might not want to follow the same route back from your objective. For example, the route might be a technical climb via a challenging route, and it makes sense to follow an easier route back. Or perhaps you have chosen to take a "scenic loop trip" on which you will never step on the same section of the route twice. Such trips can be incredibly interesting and satisfying, but require extra caution.

If you do not follow the same route on your return, be sure to carefully study the entire route beforehand, and be aware of places where you might get off the correct route. Be particularly careful of the amount of route remaining, given the pace at which you will be traveling. If there is any doubt as to whether you will be able to complete the route in the allotted time, you may have to turn around before your halfway point, or potentially hike out in the dark over unfamiliar terrain (which is not recommended).

ON THE TRAIL

When following trails, be sure to make a **mental note of all trail junctions**, or jot down such essential information as you hike, as can be done on a small notebook made of waterproof paper, which is ideal for such purposes. Some junctions are indistinct, unmarked, or obscure. Others, though marked with signs, are easy to miss if you are in a hurry or not paying close attention. When following a good trail through nondescript territory, it is easy to get into a form of mental autopilot, in which you just keep on walking without taking much note of features you are passing. In such conditions, it is easy to miss trail junctions and wander off onto the wrong trail. Try to avoid this by remaining alert to your surroundings and always searching for trail junctions and other noteworthy features.

At clearings in the forest, trail junctions, stream crossings, passes, and other known locations, **locate your position on the map** (orient yourself). Be observant of the topography that you pass, and always have the topo map available without having to remove your pack. For example, you may see a ridge or a gully coming down a mountainside, and you can glance at your map to note that you are passing such a feature. In addition to helping you to keep track of your position, this practice will eventually make you an expert map reader.

When traveling in a group, follow reasonable precautions to avoid anyone getting lost, such as assigning a responsible person known as a "sweep" to travel behind the slowest member, instructing party members to wait at important points along the way, and other measures covered in more detail in chapter 5.

When the trail becomes lost in snow, blowdowns, overgrown brush, or rocks or shale, there are still ways to find and stay on track other than just following a well-beaten trail. One way is to look for tree **blazes**—slashes, usually made by an ax (or sometimes by a paintbrush or spray paint), normally on trees about 6 feet (2 meters) or so above ground level, or on rocks on the ground. Another telltale sign are the **prunings** that occasionally are visible, where tree limbs have been cut during trail maintenance operations. If neither of these helps you to stay on the trail, ask yourself, "If I were a trail, where would I be?" Trail builders usually locate trails on the **easiest terrain**, with a minimum of ups and downs, and with the least amount of effort. Remembering this may help you to relocate the trail. If you do lose the trail in brush, woods, or snow, then you should immediately stop, retrace your steps, and locate the last known trail position. It is often tempting to keep pressing on, with the notion that the trail will eventually emerge. But this is rarely the case. **Go back and find the trail** and then start the process of finding the true route to your destination, whether back on the original trail or by some other route.

Even if the trail is muddy or full of puddles, it is strongly recommended that you **stay on the trail**, walking right through the puddles, even if it means getting your feet wet. (The inconvenience of this practice is lessened by wearing appropriate footwear: good, solid, waterproofed boots that will not soak through when you walk through water, or lightweight trail shoes that dry easily and quickly.) Walking off the trail to find dry spots eventually creates multiple parallel paths and can create a severe human impact on the wilderness. In addition, be careful not to damage trailside vegetation—for example, take rest stops at places with rocks or logs, or at open, bare areas, rather than at places where you might damage trailside vegetation. Practice sound Leave No Trace principles to **minimize the impact** of your presence.

IN THE FOREST

The moment you step off the road or trail and enter the forest, remind yourself that you are leaving your handrail, and you need to look for another one. The **new handrail** could be a topographic feature, such as a ridge, gully, or stream. In the total absence of real, physical handrails, you can conceivably follow an invisible, abstract, handrail such as a contour line (by keeping level, neither gaining nor losing elevation) or a compass bearing. If you do this, be sure to make a note of the elevation and/or bearing that you are following. Never merely wander off into the woods with no clear idea of the direction in which you are headed. You will also need a **new baseline**; this might be the road or trail that was your previous handrail.

It is best to try to **follow topographic features** when choosing a route in the forest. To avoid heavy brush, try to follow ridges and dense, old-growth timber. Gullies, watercourses, and second growth may be choked with lush, difficult vegetation. You may encounter remnants of trails from time to time. If so, take advantage of them, since doing so may save you time and energy. But keep in mind that the destination of such trails may well be different from yours, particularly if you are following game trails. If the trail starts to deviate too much from your intended direction of travel, be prepared to leave it and head back to off-trail travel.

It may sound self-evident and trite, but you should always remember that if you know where you are, you are not lost. So always **keep track of your position** using topography, time, vegetation, elevation, and any other means at your disposal. For example, you might jot down the following notes as you follow the route to your objective:

- Into woods at elev 2900 ft and bearing of 250°
- At elev 3500 ft travel level terrain at 310°
- Ascend forested ridge to broad bench at 4800 ft

Be sure to consult the map at frequent intervals to find each topographic feature that you encounter. Record your route in your notebook or on your map. Noting the direction of the slope may be of particular value in determining your position when known landmarks are obscured by forest or fog. The route will look entirely different on your return, but with the aid of your map, compass, notebook, and perhaps your altimeter or GPS device, you should be able to get back to your starting point without difficulty.

Mark the route if necessary. When traveling in the forest, it is particularly unlikely that you will follow exactly the same path on your return as on your way in, unless the topography of the area is very distinct. For this reason, it is essential to use natural materials, such as branches and logs, or biodegradable markers such as toilet paper, which deteriorates without leaving a trace.

If you have a GPS receiver, take the time at the start of your trek to **establish a waypoint** or landmark. This may be possible at the road where you leave your car. If not, then at least read the UTM coordinates off the map and enter this location as a starting point. Later, if necessary, you can establish a new position and ask the receiver to tell you the compass bearing to your starting point.

Remember to keep your map and compass handy as you travel in the forest. If you carry them in your pack, you will not use them as often as you should, since you will not want to stop frequently to remove your pack. If the route is difficult, with brush, fallen trees, or other obstacles to climb over and under, it is especially important that you not carry your compass with its lanyard around your neck, due to safety concerns. Your pocket is a far better place for it.

Enjoying the forest in the winter, early spring, or late fall can be a wonderful experience. The air is crisp and cold. Snow covers the forest floor. The bugs are gone as are the majority of travelers. However, there is one distinct disadvantage to traveling through a forest with snow obscuring the trail: the routefinding can be extremely challenging. With snow over the trail and landmarks and other objects obscured by forest, the route can be difficult to follow. Wands are very hard to follow in a forest. Further, some GPS receivers will not work well in a dense forest. The map and altimeter may be your best tools.

Begin honing your skills by traveling on snow-covered trails with which you are familiar. When en route, continually ask yourself **where you would be if you were a trail**. The moment that you are in unfamiliar terrain, retrace your route to a point at which you are familiar. If you know the direction to your destination then blaze your own trail, but do not expect that your tracks will be recognizable for the return (see "The Bootprint," later in this chapter). You may need to find a new, and better, route for the return. Keep an eye out for the trail markers, trail signage, blazes in trees, and significant landmarks on which to take compass bearings. Be on the lookout for signs of trailcraft such as sawed logs, bridges, severed limbs, and other signs of human travel or construction. Slow your pace and be diligent. Take existing footprints with a grain of salt; they are just another clue as to where the route may go. Always assume that the travelers who made the existing footprints were lost, until you prove otherwise. Reorient yourself with the smallest sign of a trail—a bridge, a trail marker, or other landmark—and, most importantly, routefind with an open mind.

IN THE DESERT

Routefinding in the desert can be easy when clear weather conditions allow you to see far-off landforms. But you should never count on such conditions. Sudden sandstorms and downpours occasionally occur, and if you are assuming that you will have good visibility for all of your routefinding you can easily get into trouble. For this reason it is crucial for you to **follow well-established trails** or other handrails, **or definite topographical features** rather than to merely assume that you can always just aim for far-off visible features.

A prime consideration for any desert travel is the **proximity to water**. A good guideline is to carry at least 1 gallon (4 liters) of water per person per day unless a dependable source of drinking water is available. There is a practical limit to how much weight you can carry, so the availability of good water along your chosen route is often a deciding factor in desert routefinding, particularly for extended trips.

The wide-open views in the desert make GPS usage easy and dependable. Under these conditions, it is most advisable to carry and frequently **use a GPS device** of some kind. (However, GPS devices do not work well, if at all, in deep canyons, for instance.) If following a poorly marked trail or dubious natural features, it might be advisable to leave your GPS receiver on continuously so as to record your exact track. If you plan on doing this, be sure to carry an extra supply of batteries, preferably longer-lasting lithium cells. You can also carry a supply of previously charged nickel-metal hydride (NiMH) recharge-able cells—a wise investment if you use a lot of battery-operated devices. Just remember to recharge them before leaving home. You might very well need them.

IN ALPINE AREAS

Many of the same suggestions offered above for forests and deserts also apply to alpine areas. First, find and follow a route using **natural topographic features** wherever possible. You can use ridges, gullies, streams, and other readily identifiable features as handrails. Even if the route appears to be obvious, pause now and then to look at the map and find your location, and observe the topographic features that you are using on your route. The sudden arrival of clouds may turn an obvious route into a challenging navigational problem. Mark your route on the map in pencil, perhaps even noting the time of arrival at various places along the route. Remember that you should be able to identify your position on the map as closely as possible at any point of your trip.

If you must deviate from natural topographic features, then use your compass to **find the bearing** that you will be following on the next leg of your trip. Make a note of this bearing in your notebook or on the map. If you have an altimeter, look at it often and follow your progress on the map. Ask yourself frequently what you would do if fog or clouds suddenly came in and obscured your view of the return route. How would you recognize key points at which you need to make crucial route changes? Should you be marking the route at such places? Should you be saving GPS waypoints?

In selecting the route, try to **minimize the impact** of your party on the terrain. Many alpine areas are particularly fragile. Some delicate woody plants, such as heather, grow only a fraction of an inch (a few millimeters) each season, and a few thoughtless footprints may wipe out an entire season's growth. If there is any trail at all, use it to minimize your impact. In the absence of a trail, try to stick to rocks, scree, talus, or snow to avoid stomping on fragile vegetation. If you must travel over alpine growth, disperse your party to minimize your personal impact as much as possible.

Open alpine areas are excellent places to use **GPS receivers**. At every rest stop, and at important route changes, take the opportunity to turn on your receiver and obtain a satellite fix. Save these locations as waypoints. In the event that you wander off route, you may be able to acquire a new position fix. Then your receiver will be able to tell you the new bearing to any of your previously established waypoints.

ON SNOW

Always be aware of potential avalanche conditions. If a slope has snow on it, then it has the possibility of sliding, often with deadly results. Slopes with a grade of about 50 percent to 170 percent (an angle of about 25° to 60°) have a high likelihood of sliding, so always **be aware of the grade of the slope**—and not just the slope you are on, but more importantly the slope above you. The most extreme hazard occurs when the slope grade is about 70 percent to 100 percent—an angle of 35° to 45°—so be particularly wary on slopes in this range. (Chapter 6 includes techniques for measuring the grade of a slope on a map, and chapter 7 explains the use of a compass's clinometer for measuring the actual angle of a slope.)

Many times you can **follow previous bootprints** in the snow to find the proper route. Even if they are several days old, an observant navigator can sometimes pick them out from sun cups and still follow the route. (Reading bootprints is covered in more detail in "The Bootprint," later in this chapter.) Vague bootprints will sometimes have a uniform indentation and may have a distinct, subtle ring of dust in them. But it is still your responsibility to know your approximate location and direction at all times. A wilderness navigator who uses the excuse "It's not my fault that we're lost—I was following tracks!" needs to read this book again before venturing out on another trek.

Following a route that has been put in on a snowfield is often academic: simply follow the bootprints. But prints are rarely permanent and can degrade quickly under some conditions. Sometimes the tracks you follow turn out to lead somewhere other than your objective. Wind and newly fallen snow can obliterate tracks, sometimes only a few seconds after they are created. The sun, especially at higher altitudes, can also erase tracks. This can be particularly surprising on a summer day when you thought that your descent following your tracks would be a piece of cake, only to find on your return trip that your footprints have melted out and have become intermingled with existing sun cups. Fortunately for the wilderness traveler, with a little homework and a few navigational tools you will be able to find your way back.

The best tools for routefinding on snow are the **map and compass**. By taking bearings on an intermediate objective such as a pass or a rock outcropping, you can navigate toward that objective even if clouds move in. If you write down those compass bearings, then on the return trip you can easily follow the back bearings for each consecutive leg and make it back. Another tool for routefinding on snow is the altimeter. The clouds have rolled in, and you press on until reaching what you hope is the summit. But a quick check of the altimeter shows that you are 700 feet (200 meters) lower than the printed summit on the map (assuming a stable barometric pressure). A look at the map shows a false summit 500 feet (150 m) lower than the true summit. It is likely that you have not quite made it yet.

A **GPS receiver** can be a big help on snow and in whiteouts. The GPS receiver can give you a pretty good idea of where you are, and where to go, but only if you have saved the proper waypoints. By entering important positions, such as the location of your camp, the receiver can guide you to your objective and back. On long trips when conserving battery power is a concern, you can obtain the proper bearing to your destination from the GPS receiver, set the bearing on your compass, and then follow it using your compass.

Capable, cautious wilderness navigators will develop the skills to use their map and compass and GPS devices, and possibly other devices (such as wands, whistles, etc.) as a complete system, rather than as independent tools.

Wands

You may occasionally have difficulty retracing your ascent route when on an indistinct snowfield where your bootprints are obliterated by wind, sun, or new snow. In this case, a dependable way to follow your ascent route is to follow tall, thin stakes called wands. Think of a set of **wands as a portable handrail** that you place on the ascent. Most

people make their own wands out of 3-foot green bamboo sticks purchased at any gardening store. Two bags of darkly stained bamboo sticks will usually yield twenty-five really good wands, once you have weeded out the flimsy and knotted ones. (Any potential wand deemed inappropriate for alpine use will happily serve its life in your garden.)

To make the wands more visible, cut a 6-inch piece of brightly colored duct tape and make a flag at the top of the stick by folding the duct tape back over itself (figure 77). To discern your wands from anyone else's, you can mark each flag with your initials and the date (e.g., MB 2015). Wands can be carried behind the compression

Figure 77. A wand with a duct tape flag

straps of your pack, where you can reach them for easy placement without removing your pack.

Wands are placed with the descent in mind, so **place wands where they will be visible on the return trip**. It is always better to place the wand on the top of a small rise rather than in a hollow. Beware of background features such as rocks or trees that can cause the wand to blend in with its surroundings. Your wands should be as easy as possible to spot and follow. One helpful trick is to angle the wand slightly toward the previously placed wand. On your return, if you cannot see the next wand, you will have a pretty good idea of the direction to it. If you still cannot see the next wand, then have the party wait at the last wand and cautiously search for the next one, always remaining in sight or within shouting distance of the rest of the party. Wait until you find the wand, and then proceed to the next one. It is all too easy for a party to rush down an indistinct snow slope and lose the wands under poor conditions. Once lost, it can be difficult to find the wanded trail again.

If the party is roped up, then a good general rule is to place the wands no farther apart than the combined length of the rope teams. If the terrain does not warrant roping up, then the safety margin must be increased and the wands placed so that you can see at least one and preferably a second wand from each successive wand. It is easiest to find successive wands if they are placed at approximately equal intervals, so that you know where and when to look for them. This might require counting paces between wands to space them at predictable intervals.

If you find that you are running out of wands, then try to supplement the wands you have by using natural terrain features. Perhaps you can place a few wands at regular intervals on an indistinct snowfield until reaching a distinct ridgeline. Then you can follow the ridgeline without placing any wands until its end. At this point you may elect to build a small temporary cairn to mark the route. Another way to conserve wands is to set one wand in a good spot, then take a compass bearing toward your previous wand and place a second wand about a foot (30 cm) from the last one, with the wands lined up to point toward the previous one. To follow the course back, simply take the compass bearing that the two wands create and follow that bearing to the previous wand(s). In this way you can place pairs of wands farther apart than single wands.

The party should always **carry enough wands** to make it to the destination. The number of wands depends greatly on the length and complexity of the route. It is not uncommon for a party to carry a hundred wands for a long route. If you are in a party of four, that is only twenty-five wands per person.

Wands left behind are considered litter. Always be sure to **remove all your wands on the descent**. Conversely, never remove someone else's wands, since they are depending on them for their descent. If you encounter someone else's wand that has melted out of the snow and has fallen over, place it upright again. Do not expect to follow somebody else's wands. They may remove them on the descent ahead of you, leaving you stranded. You and your party should be responsible for getting to and from your destination using your own resources.

It is possible that you may run out of wands before you reach your destination. Perhaps the conditions warrant more wands than you had anticipated. If this is the case, the party must decide a proper course of action. Perhaps you can use another form of navigation, such as taking a bearing from the last placed wand toward your known destination. Careful study of the map or an altimeter reading may help. Perhaps a GPS receiver can show you the way. Remember that the GPS receiver is not a panacea. It may not be accurate enough to indicate the position of your last placed wand.

ON GLACIERS

As the route ascends high above tree line and onto snowfields, the route-finding becomes easier. Snow covers the talus and protects the fragile meadows. But a new hazard may be lurking underneath: crevasses. Many times there is a traditional roping up point that divides the nontechnical ascent from the technical. At other times, in the absence of a terminal or lateral moraine, and especially in early season, it may be difficult to determine exactly where the snowfield ends and the glacier begins. Find your position on the map, and check your elevation as indicated on your altimeter or GPS device. Does your map show that you are on a glacier—a white area with a dashed blue boundary line and blue contour lines? (Note that some glaciers have boundaries that may have changed since the map was last updated, so do not trust such dashed lines if using an old map.) **Rope up for all glacier travel!** This next section assumes that you are tied in to the climbing rope.

The tools and techniques used for routefinding on snow can be used on glaciers as well. You will have two primary concerns while traveling on glaciers. One is that the route is **as efficient as possible**, as straight a line as the team can handle, leading to your objective. The second, and sometimes contradictory concern is that the route should **avoid objective hazards** such as below major icefall areas, cornices, melt streams, bergschrunds, and avalanche slopes, and should travel over as few crevasses as possible.

Many times, just as on snow, a **previous route** can be followed. Often, on popular glacier routes, the route will be a well-paved "trail" along the glacier surface. Sometimes it is so good that it forms a veritable pathway, making an otherwise steep and tricky traverse an easy walk.

Occasionally, if the route is old or if it is late in the season, it will end at a gaping crevasse, the sign of a collapsed snow bridge. A new route will have to be made over or around the crevasse in order to continue. Always be prepared to put in the route yourself.

Crevasses tend to be most plentiful around turns and obstructions and near the sides of the glacier. Often, the center of the glacier may have a more homogeneous bedrock base and thus fewer, albeit deeper, crevasses. Crevasses tend to form in groups with their attitude perpendicular to the direction of glacier flow.

Sometimes, if there is a crevasse that has just begun to show itself, a previous party may have placed two wands together forming an X. This is a warning to *steer clear*—a crevasse is probably looming underneath the snow surface. The proper way to travel around a known crevasse is to steer wide around it, a route called an **end-run**. Oftentimes on a glacier, a crevasse will exist beneath an otherwise unexplained dip in the snow surface. As you approach, keep the climbing rope taut and probe the snow deeply with your ice ax, and look through the hole to see if there is a crevasse. Step wide over the dip. Tread lightly and step over anything that you suspect may be a crevasse. Remember too that if you are putting in the route, then it is likely that many more will follow your path, perhaps even in your very footsteps. You should craft a route that is manageable for all wilderness travelers, not just for the long-legged or athletic.

While ascending, **keep the descent path in mind**. If you jump over a crevasse with uneven side walls, be sure that all party members will be able to jump over it again on the descent. Additionally, you want your route to last for several days, not hours, and summertime glacier surface melt is often significant, up to several inches per day. For this reason it is best to make long end-runs and cross on thick snow bridges.

Most prudent summit attempts on glacier routes are begun a few hours **before the coolest part of the day**. With a cold air temperature, snow bridges are firmer and the glacier surface is more likely to be frozen over, making for smooth cramponing, instead of slushy postholing. Time your start so that your descent is completed well before the heat of the day. It is common for summit teams to leave high camp between midnight and four o'clock in the morning, summit, and return to high camp before noon.

With a large party on an unblazed glacier route, it may be advantageous to send a scouting party ahead to put in the route. Alternatively, a small side trip might yield an excellent vantage point from which to view the glacier from a distance. At such a point you may more easily see the big picture of where the route should be heading as well as any major obstacles, such as icefalls, that must be avoided.

MOATS AND BERGSCHRUNDS

The area between moving snow and ice masses and stationary features like rock ridges, moraines, and summit ice caps is often defined by the existence of a moat or bergschrund.

Moats form when rock, radiated by the sun, warms and melts the snow near it. Moats can be dozens of feet deep and can be difficult to see from below. Moats have a propensity to swallow up ankles, legs, unsecured equipment, and sometimes climbers. If you are on a snow surface approaching a rock feature, always assume that a moat is lurking. As you approach the rock, probe the snow with your ice ax and look through the hole to see if the rock is visible. Step wide over the gap. It may be advantageous to cross the precipice laterally or even downhill to get a wider stride.

Bergschrunds commonly occur high on a mountain face. They are formed when the moving ice or snow mass separates from the summit ice or rock. Early in the season they may be filled in with snow and crossing them may be academic; you may not even notice them. But later in the season they can present challenging routefinding problems. Sometimes a snow bridge may cross a bergschrund. Other times the safest course is to steer wide around them, perhaps even climbing on the smooth rock at its end. Deep and wide bergschrunds can present such a significant routefinding obstacle that the team may have to turn back. There is not always a way around them.

THE BOOTPRINT

Every bootprint tells a story. **Bootprints can tell you a lot** about who and when someone has walked the path before you. As you travel, pay attention to who is in front of you and what type of prints they are leaving. Pay attention to the size, direction, and depth of the print, the shape of the sole, the distance between prints, and the style of the tread pattern. Was the person who left those prints tall or short? Was the person wearing a big, heavy pack, causing deep prints? Or was he or she wearing tennis shoes? Do you know what your own bootprint looks like? Could you follow it back after other people have made new prints on top of it?

How can you tell if you are the first travelers of the day on any particular route? Well, if the only prints that you see are facing you and look like they may have been made the previous day, then chances are that you are the only ones up there.

How far ahead is the next person? In the forest, if the tracks that you are following are filling in with water from a puddle, then the hiker is right around the corner. If the prints have fir or pine needles or leaves on them, then they are older. If the tracks in the mud are drying and becoming less defined, then the party must be at least a few hours ahead of you.

How does the energy level of your teammates measure up? If someone is ahead of you and wearing crampons, then you can make very specific observations about their gait. Are there two long parallel streaks leading to the rear crampon marks? This may indicate a party member who is getting tired. The important point here is to **be aware**. Use all the information that is available, not just what is obvious.

Once, a large group was ascending a trail. One member had to stop to make a clothing adjustment. He told everyone to continue on. One other experienced party member waited with him. The two began to follow after a few minutes. The route began to be obscured by snow, but the tracks from the party ahead were fresh and easy to follow. Then the tracks split into two different directions. Both sets of tracks were made at about the same time. (It was a popular route.) "Which way do we go?" the less experienced man asked. The more experienced man knelt down and carefully examined the two paths, without disturbing them. He reached down and touched some of the prints, testing them and seeing how the snow had formed in the spaces between where the cleats of the boot had left the prints. "They went this way," the experienced man pointed. "How do you know?" the other man asked.

The more experienced man explained that he had noticed that the last person in the group that they were following was a woman who was wearing the same style of boot that he was wearing, only it was about five sizes smaller. The odds of someone else having the same size and style of boot as that woman at that hour on that trail were low. Therefore, they went that way. All they needed to do was to follow those same prints. The two followed the unique prints and after a few minutes they caught up with their group. If the two of them had simply blundered along, unaware of the tracks that they were following, they might have

ETHIC OF SELF-RELIANCE

As mentioned in chapters 5 and 9, carrying a personal locator beacon (PLB) or satellite communicator can add a margin of safety by enabling you to initiate a rescue effort should you ever become injured, lost, or ill. However, understanding the limits of PLBs and other communication tools is as important as understanding their usefulness. Batteries deplete; electronics fail; cell phone service is limited in most wildorncoo loootiono; a rescue effort may not be possible due to weather conditions or availability of rescuers. A PLB or satellite communicator is not a substitute for self-reliance. No party should set out ill-prepared or inadequately equipped, nor should they attempt a route beyond their ability and assume that emergency help can be summoned.

missed their group's turn and might have had to double back after not finding them. But because of experience and awareness, they were able to find their group with little trouble.

Know your own bootprint. And know the bootprints of other members of your party. You may not be able to pick out every step taken along the way, but chances are you will be able to discern between ascending and descending prints, and more importantly, any changes in the prints that you are following.

CHAPTER SUMMARY

Orientation and navigation are sciences that can be easily mastered by anyone who takes the time, and makes the effort, to learn map reading and the use of the compass and other navigational tools. Practice and time spent on these subjects will enable anyone to become proficient with them. Routefinding is different. It is an art.

Some individuals seem to be born with an innate gift for finding and following a route on trails, through the forest, in the desert, in alpine regions, and on snow and glaciers. The natural abilities of such people can be greatly enhanced if they thoroughly learn the sciences of orientation and navigation, through mastery of the map, compass, and other tools. Such knowledge can enable a good routefinder to become a great one.

Some people are not blessed with great natural ability in routefinding. But there is hope for them, too. Through study and practice, they can also become proficient in orientation and navigation. They can even become experts in the use of the map and compass, if they expend the time and effort required to do so. Then, with time and experience, they can acquire much of the art of routefinding, particularly if they travel in the company of good routefinders, observing and learning as they do. Above all, there is no substitute for experience and practice.

We encourage you to reread and study this book carefully, learning the sciences of map reading, compass use, orientation and navigation, and possibly the use of other navigational tools such as the altimeter and the GPS. But this book is not enough. Repeated practice and considerable experience are necessary to thoroughly develop the skills and acquire the self-confidence that comes with repeated use of the principles described in this book. So go out into the wilderness and put the principles of *Wilderness Navigation* into practice—at first, perhaps, on good trails, then progressing to off-trail travel with ever-increasing routefinding challenges. Eventually, whether you are a natural-born routefinder or not, you can become thoroughly adept at map and compass use and will at least possess the knowledge and experience to avoid getting lost—and to recover gracefully from the experience if you ever do. And who knows, someday you might become a great routefinder, able to successfully navigate your way to any destination, solving all problems along the way, and make it back to your starting point with little difficulty or incident—because you planned it that way.

SKILLS CHECK

- List four things you can do when planning a wilderness trip that will aid you during your trip.
- What is the difference between a baseline and a handrail?
- What is a "sweep"?
- If you lose a trail in the snow, how can you find it again?
- What is a route plan?
- Why is it important to establish a turnaround time?

Bibliography

These are only a few of the many books available on the subject matter contained in this guide. These particular books (in order of usefulness) are mentioned here because they are sources of some of the information for this book, or simply because they are good books on these subjects. Other fine books on these subjects, many of which are out of print and difficult to purchase, can be found in libraries.

Mountaineering: The Freedom of the Hills, 9th edition, Mountaineers Books, 2017. *From boot selection to aid, ice, and expedition climbing techniques, this has been called the bible of the mountaineering crowd.*

Wilderness GPS: A Step-by-Step Guide, Bob Burns and Mike Burns, Mountaineers Books, 2013. *Complete information on selecting, purchasing, and using a GPS receiver for wilderness travel.*

Be Expert with Map and Compass: The Complete Orienteering Handbook, Bjorn Kjellstrom and Carina Kjellstrom Elgin, Collier Books, 2009. *Contains useful information on maps, compasses, and their use together, plus considerable information on the sport of orienteering. Latest edition of a classic book on maps and compasses.*

GPS Made Easy: Using Global Positioning Systems in the Outdoors, 5th edition, Lawrence Letham, Mountaineers Books, 2008. *Contains useful, practical instructions for using GPS receivers with UTM, latitude and longitude, and the UPS grid at the poles. Contains practical information not found in most GPS receiver instruction manuals (e.g., information on UTM).*

The Land Navigation Handbook: The Sierra Club Guide to Map and Compass, W. S. Kals, Sierra Club Books, 2010. *Basic, step-by-step instructions for using map and compass with a slightly modified Silva method. Includes direction of the slope, grade measurement, finding north with the stars in both hemispheres, and much more.*

Staying Found: The Complete Map and Compass Handbook, 3rd edition, June Fleming, Mountaineers Books, 2001. *Orientation and navigation using the method of orienting the map. Also includes finding directions with an analog wristwatch and the sun, aligning your tent to catch the morning sun, navigating with children, and more.*

Appendix: Practice Problems

All of the problems and questions on each page are to be done with reference to the map on the facing page. For measuring and plotting bearings on the map, you should assume that the solid vertical lines are aligned with north and south. The answers to all of the problems and questions are given at the end of this appendix.

1. Name the general topographic features depicted at the following points:

A _____ D _____ H _____ K _____ L _____

P _____ U _____ V _____ Z _____

2. What is the straight-line distance from point J to point X?

_____ miles _____ feet _____ meters

3. What is the distance along the road from point C to point S?

_____ miles _____ feet _____ meters

4. What are the elevations, in feet, at each of the following points?

G _____ F _____ E _____ B _____ W _____

5. What is the grade of the slope between points N and M?

6. What is the grade of the slope between points R and Q?

7. What is the general direction of the slope (fall line) at point Y?

8. What is the bearing of the slope (fall line) at point U?

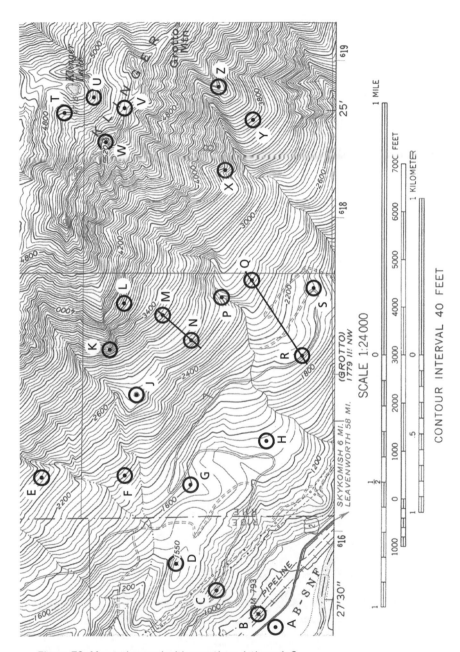

Figure 79. Map to be used with questions 1 through 8

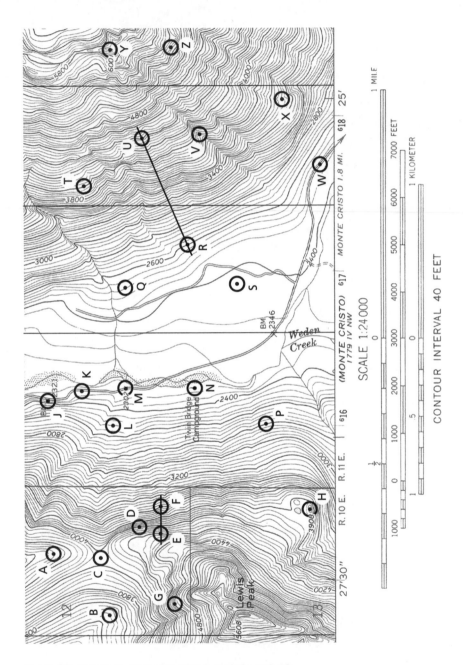

Figure 80. Map to be used with questions 9 through 16

9. Name the general topographic features depicted at the following points:

A _____ B _____ C _____ D _____ H _____ Q _____ S _____ V _____ Z _____

10. What is the straight-line distance from point J to point N?

_____ miles _____ feet _____ meters

11. What is the distance along the road from point K to point W?

_____ miles _____ feet _____ meters

12. What are the elevations, in feet, at each of the following points?

P _____ L _____ Y _____ X _____ M _____

13. What is the grade of the slope between points R and U? _____

14. What is the grade of the slope between points E and F? _____

15. What is the general direction of the slope (fall line) at point G? _____

16. What is the bearing of the slope (fall line) at point T? _____

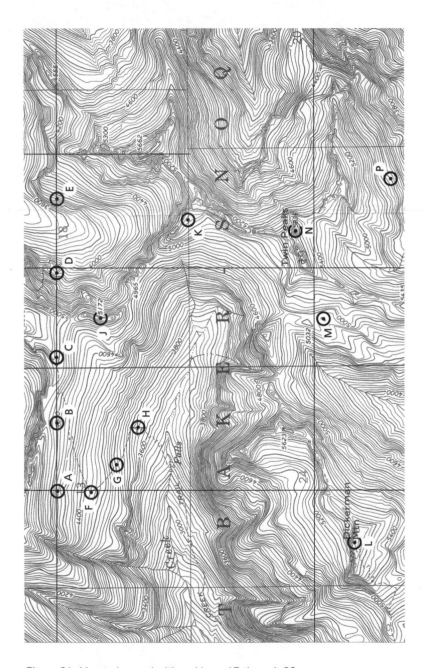

Figure 81. Map to be used with problems 17 through 23.

17. What is the bearing from point P to point M?

18. Plot a bearing of 315° from point K. Where does this plotted line intersect the horizontal line at the top of the map?

19. You are somewhere on this map, but you do not know exactly where. You take a bearing on the east peak of Twin Peaks (point N) and get 128°. You then take a bearing on Dickerman Mountain (point L) and get 207°. Where are you?

20. You are hiking along the trail in the upper left portion of this map. You wish to find out exactly where you are. You take a bearing on Peak 5172 (point J) and get a bearing of 93°. Where are you?

21. You are on the trail in the upper left part of this map. Your altimeter reads 4000 feet. Where are you?

22. From the east peak of Twin Peaks (point N), you descend to the northeast. At about what elevation do you expect to encounter a steep cliff?

23. From the summit of Peak 5172 (point J), you see a peak and take a bearing on it. You get 185°. What is the approximate elevation of this peak?

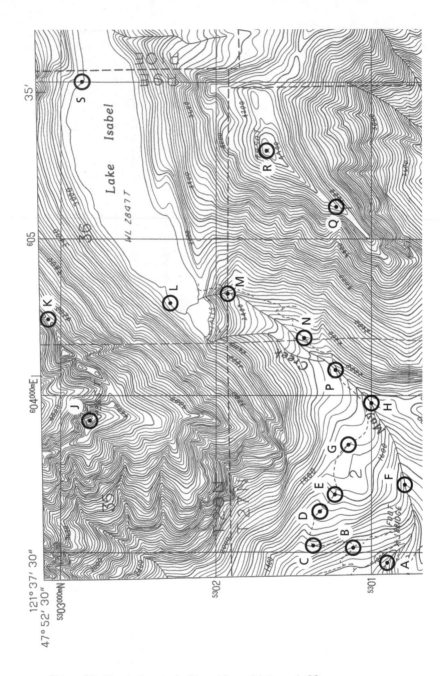

Figure 82. Map to be used with problems 24 through 30

24. What is the bearing from point S to point R? ──────

25. You are along May Creek, but you do not know exactly where. You take a bearing on Peak 4450 (point R) and get 72°. Where are you? (Indicate the letter closest to your position.) ──────

26. You take a bearing on Peak 4450 (point R) and get 78°. You take a bearing on Peak 4865 (point J) and get 17°. Where are you? (Indicate the letter closest to your position.) ──────

27. You are somewhere along May Creek. Your altimeter shows an elevation of 1320 feet. Where are you? (Indicate the letter closest to your position.) ──────

28. Your intended destination is the pass at point K. You do not know your present position. You take a bearing on point R (Peak 4450) and get 159°. You also take a bearing on point J (Peak 4865) and get 271°. What bearing should you follow to get to point K? ──────

29. You are in UTM Zone 10. You are at point L, and you turn on your GPS receiver. What is the approximate UTM reading of easting and northing that you should see on the GPS receiver? ──────

30. Your intended destination is point Q. You wish to enter this as a waypoint on your GPS receiver. What UTM coordinates would you enter on the receiver? ──────

ANSWERS TO PROBLEMS

1. A: Nearly flat area, D: Summit, H: Gentle slope, K: Cliff, L: Steep slope, P: Gully, U: Bowl (amphitheater), V: Saddle or pass, Z: Ridge
2. 0.95 mile, 5000 feet, and 1500 meters (1.5 km)
3. 2.2 miles, 11,600 feet, and 3500 meters (3.5 km)
4. G: 1600 feet, F: 2000 feet, E: 2500 feet, B: 793 feet, W: 5620 feet
5. Vertical = 400 feet. Horizontal = 800 feet. Grade = 400/800 = 0.50, or 50%
6. Vertical = 600 feet. Horizontal = 1900 feet. Grade = 600/1900 = 0.32, or 32%
7. General direction of slope (fall line) is southwest. This is the direction perpendicular to the contour lines at point Y.
8. Bearing of slope at point U is approximately 10°.
9. A: Ridge, B: Bowl or amphitheater, C: Saddle or pass, D: Cliff or very steep slope, H: Peak, Q: Gentle slope, S: Flat area, V: Gully, Z: Steep slope
10. 0.6 mile, 3200 feet, and 960 meters (0.96 km)
11. 1.5 miles, 7900 feet, and 2400 meters (2.4 km)
12. P: 2800 feet, L: 2520 feet, Y: 6001 feet, X: 3500 feet, M: 2302 feet
13. Vertical = 4400 − 2600 = 1800 feet. Horizontal = 2500 feet. Grade = 1800/2500 = 0.72 or 72%. Note that this is the average slope between these two points. From 2600 feet to about 3400 feet, it is gentler than a 72% grade. Between 3400 feet and 4400 feet, it is steeper than a 72% grade.
14. Vertical = 600 feet. Horizontal = 600 feet. Grade = 600/600 = 1.00, or 100%
15. General direction of slope (fall line) is northwest. This is the direction perpendicular to the contour lines at point G.
16. Bearing of slope at point T is about 240°.
17. 296°
18. Point C
19. Point H, at elevation 3720 feet along the trail, near a switchback
20. Point F
21. Point G
22. 4400 feet
23. 5240 feet
24. 199°
25. Point P, where the trail crosses May Creek at an elevation of about 1900 feet
26. Point E on trail
27. Point F
28. 292°
29. 10 6 04 600E; 53 02 300N
30. 10 6 05 200E; 53 01 240N

Index

Mike and Bob in Greenland in 2019

About the Authors

A longtime member of The Mountaineers, **Bob Burns** has hiked, scrambled, climbed, and snowshoed extensively in the western states and provinces of the United States and Canada. He has been teaching classes in the use of map and compass since the late 1970s, not only for Mountaineers courses but also for search-and-rescue groups, local schools, and other organizations. He is a coauthor of the navigation chapter in *Mountaineering: The Freedom of the Hills* and coauthored *Wilderness GPS* with his son, Mike.

Mike Burns is a rock, ice, and expedition climber; filmmaker; and outdoor gear consultant who has climbed throughout the Pacific Northwest, Colorado, Alaska, Canada, Mexico, Argentina, Nepal, Pakistan, and India, including a first ascent in the Himalaya. For the past thirty years he has been an instructor and lecturer on the technical aspects of climbing, section hiking, and navigation. He has written numerous articles for *The Mountaineer* and *Climbing* magazines. He is a contributor to *Mountaineering: The Freedom of the Hills* and coauthored *Wilderness GPS* with his father, Bob.

MOUNTAINEERS BOOKS

SKIPSTONE BRAIDED RIVER

recreation · lifestyle · conservation

MOUNTAINEERS BOOKS is a leading publisher of mountaineering literature and guides—including our flagship title, *Mountaineering: The Freedom of the Hills*—as well as adventure narratives, natural history, and general outdoor recreation. Through our two imprints, Skipstone and Braided River, we also publish titles on sustainability and conservation. We are committed to supporting the environmental and educational goals of our organization by providing expert information on human-powered adventure, sustainable practices at home and on the trail, and preservation of wilderness.

The Mountaineers, founded in 1906, is a 501(c)(3) nonprofit outdoor activity and conservation organization whose mission is "to explore, study, preserve, and enjoy the natural beauty of the outdoors." One of the largest such organizations in the United States, it sponsors classes and year-round outdoor activities throughout the Pacific Northwest, including climbing, hiking, backcountry skiing, snowshoeing, bicycling, camping, paddling, and more. The Mountaineers also supports its mission through its publishing division, Mountaineers Books, and promotes environmental education and citizen engagement. For more information, visit The Mountaineers Program Center, 7700 Sand Point Way NE, Seattle, WA 98115-3996; phone 206-521-6001; www.mountaineers.org; or email info@mountaineers.org.

Our publications are made possible through the generosity of donors and through sales of more than 800 titles on outdoor recreation, sustainable lifestyle, and conservation. To donate, purchase books, or learn more, visit us online:

MOUNTAINEERS BOOKS
1001 SW Klickitat Way, Suite 201 • Seattle, WA 98134
800-553-4453 • mbooks@mountaineersbooks.org • www.mountaineersbooks.org

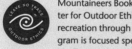 Mountaineers Books is proud to be a corporate sponsor of The Leave No Trace Center for Outdoor Ethics, whose mission is to promote and inspire responsible outdoor recreation through education, research, and partnerships • The Leave No Trace program is focused specifically on human-powered (nonmotorized) recreation • Leave No Trace strives to educate visitors about the nature of their recreational impacts and offers techniques to prevent and minimize such impacts • Leave No Trace is best understood as an educational and ethical program, not as a set of rules and regulations • For more information, visit www.lnt.org, or call 800-332-4100.